Andrew Edney

PowerPoint 2010

In easy steps is an imprint of In Easy Steps Limited
Southfield Road · Southam
Warwickshire CV47 0FB · United Kingdom
www.ineasysteps.com

Notice of Liability
Every effort has been made to ensure that this book contains accurate
and current information. However, In Easy Steps Limited and the
author shall not be liable for any loss or damage suffered by readers
as a result of any information contained herein.

Trademarks
Microsoft® and Windows® are registered trademarks of Microsoft
Corporation. All other trademarks are acknowledged as belonging to
their respective companies.

In Easy Steps Limited supports The Forest Stewardship Council (FSC),
the leading international forest certification organisation. All our titles
that are printed on Greenpeace approved FSC certified paper carry the
FSC logo.

MIX
Paper from
responsible sources
FSC® C020837

Printed and bound in the United Kingdom

ISBN 978-1-84078-405-3

Contents

1 PowerPoint 2010

This chapter will introduce you to some of the new features of PowerPoint 2010, and will begin to show you some of the different ways of doing things, including how to update PowerPoint 2010.

What is PowerPoint?

You probably already know that PowerPoint is a software package designed to help you create professional looking presentations, as easily as possible, and that it has been around for a number of years.

The latest incarnation, PowerPoint 2010, continues the tradition of providing you with all the tools you need to create and distribute your presentations, and goes that little bit further by including a number of new and exciting features, making your presentations look even more professional, with a higher quality than they had before.

PowerPoint 2010 enables you to:

- Create professional looking presentations
- Share presentations with anyone, from colleagues to customers
- Add sounds, video, pictures and more to presentations
- Create stand-alone presentations for use in kiosks, and on booths at trade shows
- Allows others to review and comment on your presentations, and even use workflow processes
- Secure your presentations using Information Rights Management technologies
- And much, much more

Microsoft Office 2010 Versions

There are a number of different versions of Microsoft Office 2010 currently available, including:

- Office Home and Student
- Office Standard
- Office Professional

Each one of the above Microsoft Office 2010 versions contains PowerPoint 2010, so it doesn't matter which version you buy, you will still get access to PowerPoint.

Microsoft have also introduced 64-bit versions of Office 2010, which you can use if you have a 64-bit version of Windows.

Hot tip

If you are running a 64-bit version of either Windows Vista or Windows 7, you should use the 64-bit version of Office 2010 in order to take full advantage of your current system.

Hot tip

Check out what comes with each version of Microsoft Office 2010, and make sure you purchase the version that is right for you.

PowerPoint Requirements

In order to be able to install and use PowerPoint 2010, you will need to ensure that your computer meets the minimum requirements for running PowerPoint 2010, which are as follows:

Component	Requirement
Processor	500 MHz Processor or higher
Memory	256 MB RAM or higher
Hard Disk	1.5 GB free
Drive	CD-ROM or DVD Drive
Display	1024 x 768 or higher resolution monitor
Operating System	Minimum Windows XP with SP3, Windows Vista, Windows 7
Other	Certain Inking features require Windows XP Tablet PC Edition or later; Speech recognition functionality requires a close-talk microphone and audio output device; Information Rights Management features requires Windows 2003 Server with SP1 or later running Windows Rights Management Service; Internet Explorer 7.0 or later; Collaboration requires Windows SharePoint Services; PowerPoint Slide Libraries require Office SharePoint Server 2010
Additional	Actual requirements and product functionality may vary based on system configuration and operating system

Hot tip

If you are planning on installing and running PowerPoint 2010, on any version of Windows 7, you should consider increasing the processor and memory to compare with that listed in the minimum requirements.

Hot tip

PowerPoint 2010 is designed to run on older versions of both Windows and older hardware platforms – you may not need to upgrade any hardware.

Beware

If you are planning on using Windows 7 as your operating system, you should ensure that your computer is capable of running the version of 7 you want to use.

New and Improved Features

PowerPoint 2010 introduces a wealth of new and improved features designed to help you to create professional looking presentations, and to get the most out of the product without you having to do every little thing yourself.

Some of these new and improved features include:

- An intuitive user interface called the Ribbon

- A new Microsoft Office Backstage view for quickly gaining access to common tasks

- Improved effects, themes and enhanced formatting options

- The ability to use a Live preview that shows you the result of what you can select, without having to actually select it

- A number of predefined Quick Styles that include layouts, table formats, effects and more

- The ability to initiate workflow processes

- Broadcasting your slide show over the Internet

- SmartArt graphics that can be used to quickly and easily produce high quality designer-style graphics

- The new XML file format, which reduces the size of the file and also provides enhanced recovery abilities

- Enhancements and improvements for tables and charts

- A Presenter View, which enables you to run your presentation on one monitor while you view something different on another monitor, this can make the task of actually delivering your presentation that much easier

- ✓The ability to save your presentations as a PDF

- A number of security-related functions, including enhanced Information Rights Management, and the ability to find and remove hidden metadata from your presentations. You can also add digital signatures to your presentations

Beware

Some of the new features require additional software, such as Microsoft Office SharePoint Server 2010, in order to make them work, and may also require additional hardware.

10

Installing PowerPoint 2010

If you have not yet installed PowerPoint 2010 then now is the time to do so.

1 Insert the Microsoft Office 2010 CD into your computer

2 If the setup program does not start automatically, double-click on setup.exe on the CD to start it

3 Click Install Now to perform a standard installation, or click Customize to select what you want to install

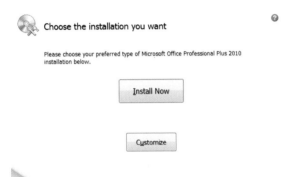

4 If you clicked on Customize, work through the available programs and select whether or not to install each one

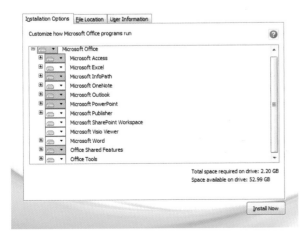

Hot tip

You can check out all of the new features of PowerPoint 2010, and other Office 2010 applications, by downloading a trial version from http://www.microsoft.com/office.

Hot tip

If you already have a version of Office installed on your computer, you may be offered the option to Upgrade your existing installation. By upgrading, you will keep all your existing settings.

Hot tip

Even if you are running a 64-bit version of either Windows Vista or Windows 7, the default version of Office 2010 installed is the 32-bit version, so make sure you install the 64-bit version.

...cont'd

Hot tip

If you want to install all of the available programs, just select Run all from My Computer when clicking on Microsoft Office.

Don't forget

Make sure you have enough available free disk space, in order to install all of the Microsoft Office programs that you have selected.

Don't forget

You will need a valid Product Key to complete the installation of Microsoft Office 2010.

5 Click on the File Location tab to select where on your computer to install the chosen Office 2010 programs

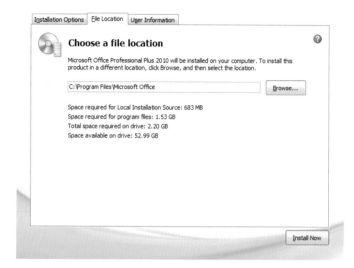

6 Click on the User Information tab and enter your details in the Full Name, Initials, and Organization boxes, then click the Install Now button

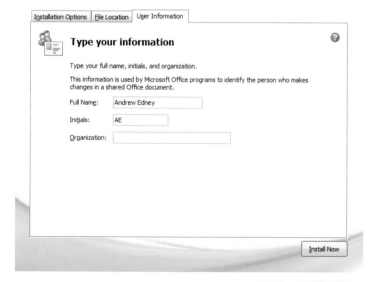

Starting PowerPoint 2010

Before you can start to create your presentations, you have to start PowerPoint 2010. There are different ways you can do this.

The Start Menu
Like any application, you can start PowerPoint by selecting it from the Start Menu.

1 Click on the Start button

2 Click on All Programs

3 Click on Microsoft Office

4 Double-click on Microsoft Office PowerPoint 2010

Microsoft LifeCam
Microsoft Mouse
Microsoft Office
   Microsoft Excel 2010
   Microsoft OneNote 2010
   Microsoft Outlook 2010
   Microsoft PowerPoint 2010
   Microsoft SharePoint Workspace
   Microsoft Word 2010
   Microsoft Office 2010 Tools

Hot tip

You can also add PowerPoint 2010 to the Quick Launch area on your desktop by dragging it there.

Creating a Shortcut
You can create a shortcut icon on your desktop, to enable you to quickly launch PowerPoint.

1 From the Start Menu, click and hold the Microsoft Office PowerPoint 2010 icon

2 Drag the mouse to the desktop and release the button to create the shortcut

Don't forget

You can also start PowerPoint 2010 by double-clicking on any PowerPoint presentation that you have access to.

Creating a New Presentation
You can create a new presentation and then launch it.

1 Click the right mouse button and click New, followed by Microsoft Office PowerPoint Presentation

2 Name the new file, then double-click on it to launch it and start creating your slides

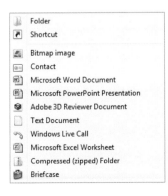

Folder
Shortcut

Bitmap image
Contact
Microsoft Word Document
Microsoft PowerPoint Presentation
Adobe 3D Reviewer Document
Text Document
Windows Live Call
Microsoft Excel Worksheet
Compressed (zipped) Folder
Briefcase

Exploring the Ribbon

Hot tip

You will notice that if you use any other Microsoft Office 2010 application, the Ribbon is included in all of them in one form or another. So, when you are used to using it, you should have no problems in other applications.

The Ribbon is the replacement for the various menus and toolbars that you may be used to, if you have used a previous version of PowerPoint before 2007. Apart from looking completely different, the Ribbon provides both contextual tabs and menus. What this means is that different options will be available to you, depending on what you are doing and what you select. This reduces the clutter of menus and toolbars you may not need very often, and provides you with the menus you need when you need to use them.

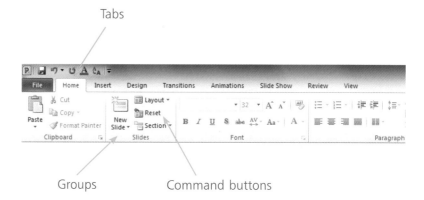

Tabs

Groups   Command buttons

Don't forget

Additional tabs will be displayed as and when they are needed, depending on what you select and what you are doing at that time.

The various commands are grouped together logically under different tabs. Each of the tabs relates to a different activity, and includes various command buttons. The initial tabs that are available for use are:

- Home – includes command groups and buttons for the clipboard, slides, fonts, paragraphs, drawing and editing, and also the new backstage view

- Insert – includes command groups and buttons for tables, illustrations, links, text and media clips

- Design – includes command groups and buttons for page setup, themes and backgrounds

- Transitions – includes command groups and buttons for transitions and timings

- Animations – includes command groups and buttons for previewing and animations

- Slide Show – includes command groups and buttons for starting slide shows, setting up slide shows and monitor settings

- Review – includes command groups and buttons for proofing, comments and protecting your presentation

- View – includes command groups and buttons for presentation views, show/hide functions, zoom, color/grayscale use, windows and using macros

There are two additional type of tabs that can appear when they are needed – Contextual tabs and Program tabs.

Hot tip

If you need to hide the Ribbon at any time, just press CTRL + F1 to hide it, and then press CTRL + F1 again to restore it.

Contextual Tabs

Contextual tabs appear when you select an object, such as a picture or text box. Depending on what you select, a contextual tab will appear. For example, if you select a text box, the Drawing Tools tab will appear.

Contextual tab

Minimizing the Ribbon

If you decide that you don't want the Ribbon to be visable, you can easily hide it by clicking on the Minimize the Ribbon button.

Minimize the Ribbon button

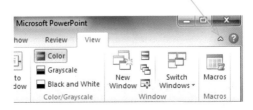

2003 Commands in 2010

If you are familiar with using PowerPoint 2003, then you will probably notice that PowerPoint 2010 looks completely different. If you have ever used PowerPoint 2007, you will probably notice that it looks very similar, although certain features have changed locations, or had tabs added for ease of use, and some things have been completely replaced, such as the Microsoft Office Button. A major difference is that some of the commands you might be comfortable using are either no longer there, or are not obvious as to their location.

There are a few different ways to familiarize yourself with the 2010 commands. One very useful tool, that Microsoft provides, is an Interactive PowerPoint 2010 command reference guide.

Hot tip

There are also many different websites offering hints, tips and tricks on using PowerPoint 2010, if you are only used to an earlier version. Use your favorite Internet search engine to find them.

1 From your Internet browser, go to: http://office2010. microsoft.com/en-gb/powerpoint-help/learn-the-ribbon-and-backstage-view-HA101794130.aspx?CTT=5&origin =HA010359435&redir=0

2 Click the Start the guide button

3 When the guide begins, you can work your way through it and learn the location of all of your favorite commands

4 If you want to have the Interactive guide available to you when you are not connected to the Internet, or for when you are travelling, you can download it

There are also Menu to Ribbon Reference Workbooks available. These workbooks provide a comprehensive list of all of the menu and toolbar commands, and their locations on the ribbon or in the Backstage view.

1 Download the Menu to Ribbon Reference Workbook

2 When you open the workbook it will open in Excel, so you will need to have Excel installed to view it

Backstage View

If you are familiar with previous versions of PowerPoint, or other Microsoft Office applications, you will have used the File menu at some point, to save, print or perform any number of possible tasks.

PowerPoint 2010 introduces the Backstage view. This appears in the upper-left corner on all Microsoft Office 2010 applications as the File tab.

1 To open the Backstage view, click on the File tab.

The File Tab

Hot tip

You can shut down PowerPoint from this menu by clicking on the Exit button.

2 Click on whichever menu item you want to use, or that you want to expand

3 Click on the item in the box that you want to use, for example, Manage Versions

Quick Access Toolbar

The Quick Access Toolbar is a toolbar that is completely customizable by you, to include any commands that you might use on a regular basis, such as Save or Print. Rather than work your way through the menus, you can just click the relevant command on the Quick Access Toolbar to activate the command.

Quick Access Toolbar

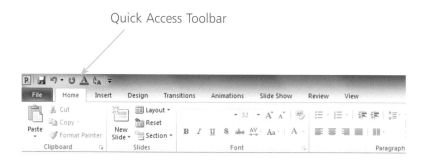

Hot tip

By default, the Quick Access Toolbar appears above the Ribbon. You can have it appear below the Ribbon by selecting Show Quick Access Toolbar Below the Ribbon, when right-clicking the Quick Access Toolbar.

Customizing the Quick Access Toolbar

You can add or remove commands from the Quick Access Toolbar whenever you need to. There are a few different ways of adding commands.

1. Highlight the command you want to add to the Quick Access Toolbar

2. Click on the right mouse button, and select Add to Quick Access Toolbar from the menu

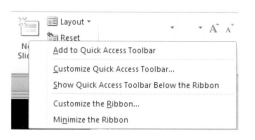

Hot tip

You can quickly remove a command from the Quick Access Toolbar, by right-clicking it from the Toolbar and selecting Remove from Quick Access Toolbar.

Another way involves you selecting from a list of the commands within PowerPoint 2010, and then choosing whichever one you want to add to the Quick Access Toolbar, from the Customize menu of Options from the Backstage view.

1 Click on the File tab and select the Options button

2 Click on Customize Ribbon

Hot tip

You can also launch the Customize menu by selecting Customize Quick Access Toolbar when you right-click on any command.

Hot tip

You can customize the Quick Access Toolbar for all of your PowerPoint 2010 presentations (which is the default setting), or you can choose to only customize the toolbar for the current presentation.

3 Click on the Choose commands from the drop-down list, then select which area you want to display the commands for

4 Scroll through the commands and click on the command you want to add, then click the Add button

5 Repeat steps 3 through 5 until you have added all of the commands you want to the Toolbar

Hot tip

Don't worry if you make a mistake, you can just click on the Reset button to restore the Quick Access Toolbar to its default setting.

6 Use the up and down arrows to reorder the commands in the Quick Access Toolbar list until you are happy, then click the OK button to finish customizing the Quick Access Toolbar

Help and How-to

If you experience a problem, or would like some help on how to do something particular with PowerPoint 2010, then help is literally at hand. PowerPoint has a detailed help and how-to component, and, when you are connected to the Internet, this is expanded to include additional content and anything else new.

1 Click on the Help button on the Ribbon (its the ?) near the top right-hand corner of the screen

2 Click on any entry to see additional topics

3 Click on one of the newly displayed topics to see the help or how-to information for that particular topic

4 Click the Print icon if you want to print it

5 Click the Back icon to return to the list, or click the Home icon to return to the start

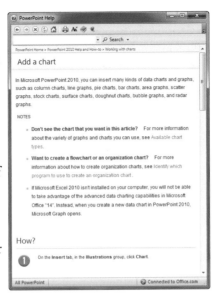

Hot tip

You can refine the search type by clicking on the arrow on the Search button and choosing a type that suits your search criteria, such as only searching PowerPoint Training.

21

Manual Searching

You can also enter text into the search box to look for something specific, instead of trying to find it from the various lists.

1 Enter a word, phrase or text entry into the search box

2 Click the Search button to begin the search

Beware

If you are searching Office Online, you will also see results for other Office applications and different versions of PowerPoint (unless you consider refining your search).

Search Locations

You can choose to search for content from Office Online, or only from the local computer.

1 Click the Connection Status box and select the location

Office Online

The Microsoft Office Online website provides a wealth of useful tools, guides, downloads and more, that are invaluable to any Microsoft Office user.

To access certain online services content, you will need to register on the site.

1 Click the File tab and select Options

2 Click on Help and then select the Getting Started button from the go to Microsoft Office Online

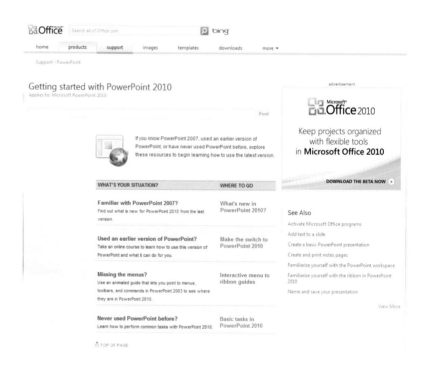

3 Click on any of the resources you would like to access

4 Some resources may require you to sign-in with your Windows Live ID

Updating PowerPoint 2010

It is very important that you keep PowerPoint 2010, and all of your Microsoft Office applications, up to date. Updates are released periodically, they include bug fixes and product updates, so there may be something that you need. One of the simplest ways to update Office is to have Office check for updates for you.

1 Click the File tab and select Options

2 Click on the Help area

3 Click on Check for updates

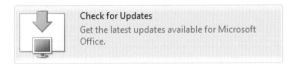

Using Windows Update

The simplest, and easiest way by far, is to use Windows Update and allow it to manage all of your updates, including Microsoft Office and Windows 7. To use Windows Update, just click on Windows Update in Windows 7 and follow any prompts.

Beware

Never let your application or operating system become out of date, as this could potentially leave you vulnerable to viruses and other malicious code, not to mention application problems.

23

Hot tip

You can install Microsoft Update by clicking on the Get updates for more products button, which appears on the Windows Update screen. Follow the on-screen prompts to complete the installation.

KeyTips

You may not want to use the mouse to select items from the Ribbon, or you might want to use some of the keyboard shortcuts that are available to speed up your work.

These keyboard shortcuts are known as KeyTips and are used to access a tab, or to perform a function, by pressing a single key or series of keys from your keyboard.

1   Press and release the ALT key at anytime

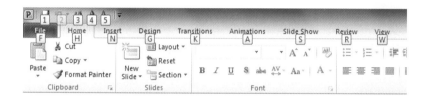

2   Press the key that matches the action you want to perform, such as W for the View tab

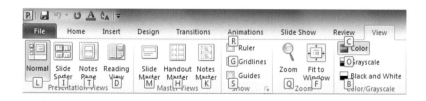

3   Press the ALT key again to cancel the KeyTips selection

Other Keyboard Shortcuts

Apart from the KeyTips, there are numerous keyboard shortcuts that can be used within PowerPoint 2010.

For a detailed list of the shortcuts, and their functions, do a search for Keyboard Shortcuts for PowerPoint 2010 from the Office Help area. You should then be able to select the help document that contains the list.

2 Creating Presentations

This chapter will explain how to begin to create a new PowerPoint presentation, how to use templates and existing presentations, and also start to show off some of the features.

The Workspace

The Workspace is where you will work with PowerPoint 2010, so it is important that you understand what each part is called and what it is used for.

The Slide Pane
This is where you will do all of your work in creating your presentations.

Placeholders
Placeholders are the dotted boxes and are used to add text, graphics, and other items into your presentation.

26

The Slides Tab   The Slide Pane

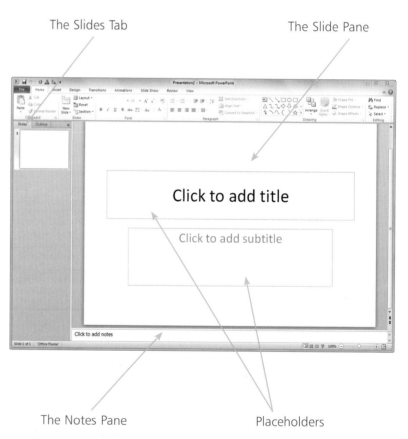

The Notes Pane   Placeholders

The Slides Tab
This includes views of your slides, with the current slide being highlighted.

The Notes Pane
This is where you can add notes to your presentations.

Starting a Presentation

When you first start PowerPoint 2010 you are presented with the title page to a blank presentation, which you can use to start creating your own presentation immediately.

1 To add a title, click the Click to add title placeholder and type in the title you want to use

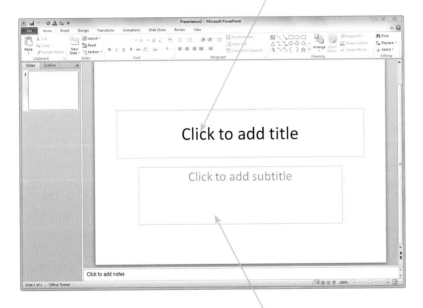

Don't forget

Whatever notes you type will not appear when you are delivering your presentation, but you can include them when you print or export your presentation for others to view.

2 To add a subtitle, click the Click to add subtitle placeholder and type in the text that you want to use

3 If you want to make some notes, you can do so by clicking on the Click to add notes text box and typing in whatever you want to appear in the Notes view later

4 You can move the position of the placeholders around by clicking and dragging them to a new position

You can also change the background or theme, add graphics, shapes, more text, and more, all of which will be covered throughout this book.

Slide Layouts

When you first start PowerPoint you will see the Title Slide layout, but there are a number of other predefined layouts that you can choose from, and use in your presentations on any slide.

These predefined layouts include:

- Title and Content
- Title Only
- Blank
- Picture with Caption

You can select any of these at any time, just click in the placeholders that are provided to easily create a slide, with the exception of the Blank layout, which enables you to effectively start from scratch and create whatever look you want for the slide.

1   Ensure the Home tab is selected

2   From the Slides group, click on the Layout button

3   Select the layout you want

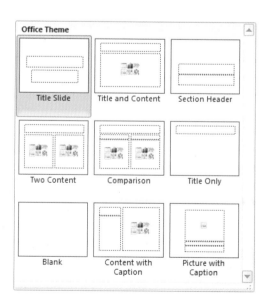

Adding Slides

You can add a new slide at any time by just clicking on the New Slide button on the Slides group.

1 Ensure the Home tab is selected

2 From the Slides group, click on the New Slide button

3 Select the layout you want by clicking on it

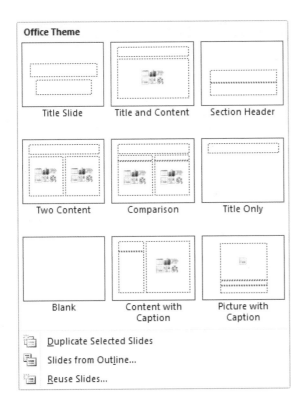

Office Theme

Title Slide

Title and Content

Section Header

Two Content

Comparison

Title Only

Blank

Content with Caption

Picture with Caption

Duplicate Selected Slides

Slides from Outline...

Reuse Slides...

Duplicating Slides

You can make a complete copy of a slide, including any content that appears on it, so that you don't have to spend time recreating a certain look or feel, and then you can just amend anything on the slide itself.

Hot tip

If you want to add the same type of slide you recently added, just click on the Slide icon, rather than New Slide, to repeat the previous addition.

Hot tip

You can also duplicate slides by highlighting them from the Slides view and pressing CTRL + C to copy then CTRL + P to paste.

...cont'd

Hot tip

You can also browse for a presentation, or type in the full path to the presentation.

1 Select the slide or slides from the Slides view that you want to duplicate

2 On the Home tab, click New Slide from the Slides group

3 Click on Duplicate Selected Slides

Reusing Slides

You can now reuse slides from other presentations, or from published slides in a slide library.

Don't forget

If you want to use a slide from a Slide Library, you will need to ensure you have access to that Slide Library.

1 On the Home tab, click New Slide from the Slides group

2 Click on Reuse Slides

3 If you want to use a slide that is published in a Slide Library, click on Open a Slide Library and enter the URL of the Slide Library

4 If you want to use a slide from an existing presentation, click on Open a PowerPoint File

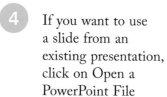

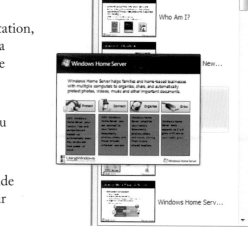

5 Select the presentation you want to use

6 Click on the slide to add it to your presentation

Hot tip

For details on how to publish your slides to a Slide Library, take a look at Chapter 11 – Sharing Presentations.

Views

There are a number of different views available to you that you might find very useful.

Normal View
Normal View is the standard PowerPoint 2010 view that appears whenever you start PowerPoint. In Normal View you can also see either the Slides View or the Outline View alongside the main presentation window.

Hot tip

The Outline view will be covered in Chapter 8 – Reviewing & Proofing.

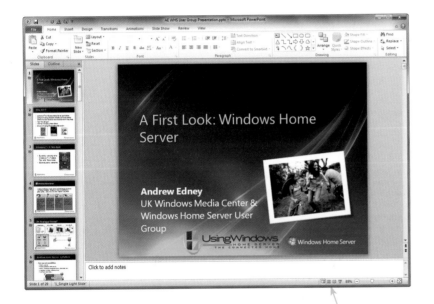

Hot tip

You can easily switch between Normal Slides view and Normal Outline view by clicking on the relevant tab.

Changing Views
The different views can be selected by clicking on the View buttons that are located at the bottom of the presentation window.

Normal   Slide Show

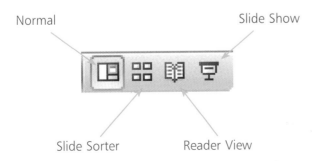

Slide Sorter   Reader View

Hot tip

The Slide Sorter view and Slide Show view will be covered in Chapter 9 – Creating Slide Shows.

Zoom Slider

You can zoom in and out of the presentation window by using the Zoom Slider control, which is located at the bottom of the presentation window.

1 Click the - or + symbols on the zoom slider to decrease or increase the presentation window size; or

2 Drag the zoom slider button to a new position

Hot tip

Use the Zoom Slider to get the view in as close as you need to, in order to assist you in trying to line up objects precisely.

3 Click the Fit slide to current window button, to fill the presentation window, if you want to do that

Before fitting slide to current window

After fitting slide to current window

Page Layout and Orientation

The page layout and orientation you use for your slides, and your presentation, is very important. Depending on how you deliver your presentation, you may have a specific need to present the slides in portrait rather than the default layout, which is landscape.

1 Click on the Design tab

2 Click on Page Setup

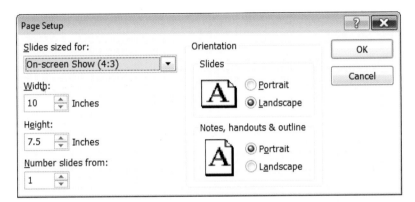

33

3 Select what medium the slides should be sized for from the drop-down list

4 Select the width and height, in inches

5 Set the orientation for the slides, and also for any notes, handouts and outlines

6 Click OK

Changing the Slide Orientation Only

1 Click on Slide Orientation

2 Select either Portrait or Landscape

Templates and Themes

PowerPoint 2010 comes packed full of templates and themes that you can use to get your presentation started. You can then add to or change the presentation as you begin to develop it.

1 Click on the File tab

2 Click New from the menu

3 You can start from a blank presentation, or select from recently used templates and themes by clicking on the presentation you want to use

34

4 To select from one of the many installed Themes, click on Themes and select the theme you want to use

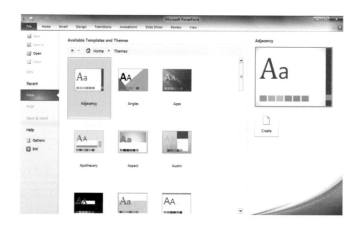

5 To select from one of the many installed Templates, click on Sample Templates and select the template you want

6 Click Create to create a new presentation based on your selection

7 If you have saved any templates yourself, you can select them by clicking on My templates

8 Select the template you want to use and click OK

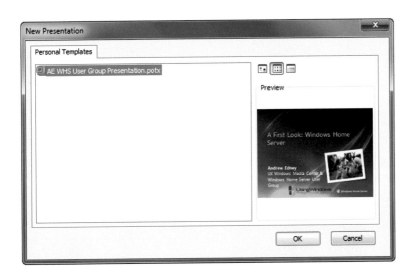

Hot tip

To add a template to the My Templates area, you need to have saved it as a PowerPoint Template.

Downloading Presentations

You can also choose from a large amount of content that is hosted on Microsoft Office Online. To make your selection easier, this additional content is sorted into a number of different categories, including:

- Diagrams and Plans

- Presentations (including some training presentations for Office 2010)

- Reports

- And much more

1 Click on the Office.com Templates type, choose the template type you are interested in, then click on the template you want

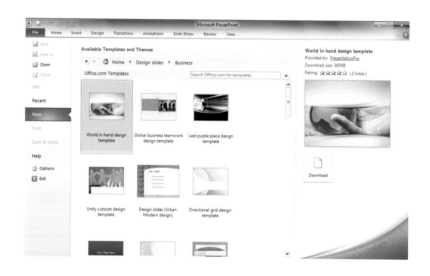

2 Click the Download button to download the content

3 You may be asked to confirm that your copy of Microsoft Office is genuine, click Continue if you are to begin the checking process

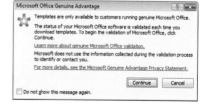

Don't forget

You will need to be connected to the Internet in order to download content from Microsoft Office Online.

Hot tip

Check Microsoft Office Online regularly, as new content is added all the time and something might appear that you are interested in.

Beware

If Windows Genuine Advantage fails to confirm the authenticity of your installed Office application, you should contact Microsoft immediately and obtain a genuine copy.

Creating Custom Layouts

If you find that none of the layouts quite suit what you require,
you can always create your own custom layout, which you can
then use whenever you need to. You can add many different types
of placeholders to the custom layout, and choose any location on
the slide where you want them to appear.

1 Click on the View tab, and in the Master Views group
select Slide Master

2 Scroll to the bottom of the slide master and layouts, then
click below the last entry

3 Click on Insert Layout from the Edit Master group

Hot tip

Before starting to create
a new custom layout in
PowerPoint, you could
consider drawing it on
some paper, just to get
an idea of what you
want it to look like.

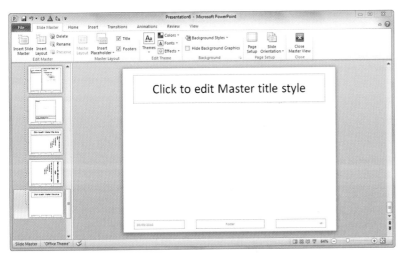

...cont'd

Hot tip

You could also remove the default placeholder by unchecking the Title box from the Master Layout group.

Hot tip

You can resize any of the placeholders by dragging one of the corners to the size you want it to be.

Hot tip

Once it has been created and saved, the new layout can be selected from the Layout menu on the Slides group.

4 If you want to remove the default placeholder, click the border of the placeholder and press DEL on your keyboard

5 If you do not want footers to appear on your slide layout, uncheck the Footers box from the Master Layout group

6 To start to add your placeholders, click on the Insert Placeholder button from the Master Layout group

7 Select the type of Placeholder that you want to add

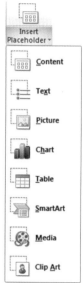

8 Click and hold the mouse button at the location on the layout where you want the chosen placeholder to start, and then just drag it across the layout until you are happy with the size, then release the button

9 Repeat steps 7 and 8 for each Placeholder you want to add to the new layout

Click to edit Master title style

- Click to edit Master text styles
  - Second level
    - Third level
      - Fourth level
        » Fifth level

- Table

- SmartArt graphic

- Media

2/18/2007   Footer

10 Save the new layout as a PowerPoint template, then click Close Master View to finish

Opening Presentations

You can open presentations from the current version of PowerPoint, or from previous versions.

1 Click on the File tab

2 If the presentation you want to open has been opened recently, click on Recent and you can select it from there

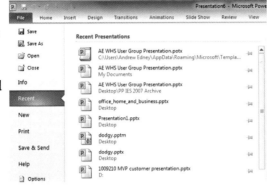

3 If not, click on Open

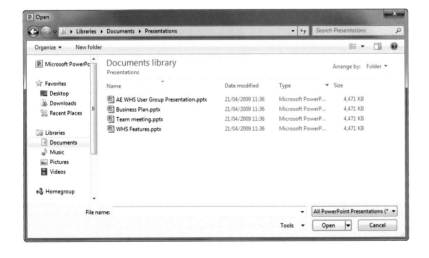

4 Search for the presentation file you want to open

5 Either double-click it, or click it once and then click Open

Hot tip

If you open a presentation from a previous version of PowerPoint, it is opened in Compatibility Mode – more on that on the next page.

Hot tip

If you want a presentation to always appear in the Recent Documents list, regardless of when you last opened it, you can Pin It to the list by clicking the pin icon next to the name. When the pin turns green it is pinned. Gray means it is unpinned.

Hot tip

If you click on the Open button arrow you will be presented with a number of options for opening the file, including Open as Copy and Open and Repair, if the file is damaged.

Converting Presentations

If you open a presentation that was created with an earlier version of PowerPoint, it will open in what is known as Compatibility Mode. Compatibility Mode is used to suppress certain functionality within PowerPoint 2010 in order for you to be able to continue to work on and share the presentation with users of that earlier version of PowerPoint. Examples of the suppressed functionality can include:

- SmartArt Graphics
- Certain Quick Styles and Text Effects

You can tell you are in Compatibility Mode because [Compatibility Mode] is displayed next to the file name.

Business Plan.ppt [Compatibility Mode] - Microsoft PowerPoint

You can convert the presentation to a PowerPoint 2010 format and enable all of the suppressed functionality.

Hot tip

For more information about compatibility and saving for different versions of PowerPoint, see Chapter 10 – Saving Your Presentation.

40

Beware

Once you have converted the presentation to a PowerPoint 2010 format, you will not be able to share it with users of previous versions of PowerPoint, without saving it in a previous version.

1. Open the presentation that was created with an earlier version of PowerPoint

2. Click on the File tab

3. Select Convert, from the Info menu

Close

Info

Recent

Convert

Compatibility Mode
Some new features are disabled for improved compatibility with previous versions of PowerPoint. Upgrading to the current file format will enable these new features. Affected objects include charts, diagrams, and media objects.

4. Choose a location and save the newly converted presentation file

3 Working with Text

This chapter will explain how to add and format text for use in your presentations, and how to use WordArt to make your presentations look even better.

Text

One of the main elements to your presentation is likely to be text – whether you are using text for different types of titles, lists or paragraphs, or a mixture of the three.

Adding Text to a New Slide

If you choose to create a new slide, and select a layout that includes any sort of text box, you can just click on the text box and enter whatever text you want to appear.

1 To add a title, click on the Click to add title box placeholder and enter the text you want to use

2 To add a subtitle, click on the Click to add subtitle box placeholder and enter the text you want to use for the subtitle

> **Click to add title**
>
> Click to add subtitle

Adding a Text Box Placeholder to a Slide

You can also add a text box placeholder anywhere on the slide, and enter any text you want into that box.

1 Click on the Insert tab and from the Text group, click on Text Box

2 Position the mouse pointer where you want to start drawing the text box, hold down the left mouse button and drag the box to the size you want, then release the mouse button

3 Enter the text in the box

This is a text box

Hot tip

You can also copy an existing text box placeholder, by selecting it and pressing CTRL + C and then CTRL + V to paste it. You can then move it to any position on the slide and edit it.

AutoFit

If you have entered more text into a text placeholder than the placeholder can actually contain, you may have noticed that the text you entered automatically resizes to a smaller font in order to fit all of the text into the placeholder. This function is called AutoFit and can be very useful in ensuring that everything you want to enter into a text placeholder is actually displayed. This works by first reducing the amount of line spacing, and then reducing the font size.

1 If you are entering some text and you fill up the placeholder, the Autofit Options button will appear

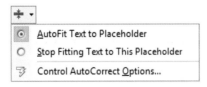

The Year End Results for Fiscal Year 2007 and the plan for year 2008

43

2 If you want to AutoFit the text to the placeholder, just keep typing and it will be automatically adjusted

3 If you do not want to AutoFit the text, click on the AutoFit Options button

⊙	AutoFit Text to Placeholder
○	Stop Fitting Text to This Placeholder
⍢	Control AutoCorrect Options...

4 Click the Stop Fitting Text to This Placeholder

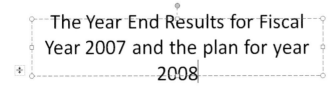

The Year End Results for Fiscal Year 2007 and the plan for year 2008

Formatting Paragraphs

You may want to format the text you have entered by changing its alignment, its indentation, its line spacing, its direction and more. The place to make all these formatting changes is from the Paragraph group, which is located on the Home tab.

1 Select the text you want to format

2 Click on the Home tab

3 If you want to increase or decrease the indent level, click the indent buttons

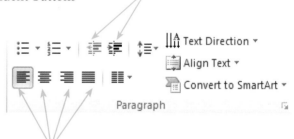

4 Click the alignment buttons to change the alignment, or to justify the text

5 If you want to adjust the line spacing, you can either click the Line Spacing button and select a value, or you can select Line Spacing Options to set your own values

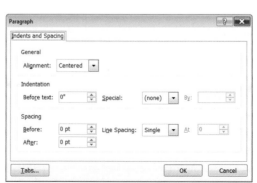

6 Make the adjustments to General, Indentation and Spacing, then click on OK to finish

Changing Text Direction

You can change the direction of the text by selecting one of the preset options from the Text Direction menu.

1. Select the text you want to change

2. Click on the Home tab

3. From the Paragraph group, click the Text Direction button

4. Select the direction of the text from the available choices

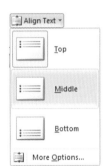

Aligning the Text

1. This time choose the Align Text button from the Paragraph group

2. Select the alignment of the text from the available choices

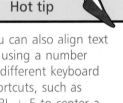

More Options

Once again, you can make adjustments to create a more specific change.

1. From either the Text Direction menu or the Align Text menu, select More Options

2. Adjust the settings that are available from this dialog box

3. Click Close

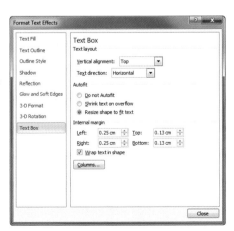

Hot tip

You can also align text by using a number of different keyboard shortcuts, such as CTRL + E to center a paragraph, CTRL + J to justify a paragraph, CTRL + L to align left and CTRL + R to align right.

Fonts

There are numerous different fonts that you can use in your presentation. You can change the font for a single word, a slide, or the whole presentation itself.

Changing the Font on a Single Slide

1 Highlight the word or text you want to change

2 Click on the Home tab, if you are not already on it

3 Click on the Font list arrow in the Font group to display all the available fonts

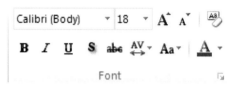

4 Scroll through the list of fonts and select the one you want to use

You will notice that the text you highlighted automatically changes as you scroll through each of the different fonts.

Changing the Font Throughout the Presentation

If you want to change the font throughout your whole presentation, you can access the Slide Master and change the fonts within the theme. Alternatively, you can use the Replace Fonts feature of PowerPoint 2010. In order to use this feature, you may need to add it to the Quick Access Toolbar.

$^{A}_{A}$ Replace Fonts...

1 Click on the Replace Fonts button

2 Choose the font you want to replace, from the Replace drop-down list

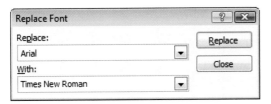

3 Choose the font you want to replace the font with, from the With drop-down list

4 Click the Replace button

Formatting the Font

You can format any selected text, to change the size of the font, the color, and even to add various effects, such as strikethrough.

1 Select the text that you want to format

2 Click on the Home tab and then click the Font dialog box launcher

3 Make changes to the font, style, size and color

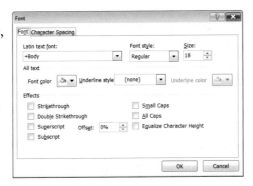

4 Check any Effects boxes, to add the effects to the text

5 Click OK

47

WordArt

PowerPoint 2010 has a collection of different text styles that you can use in your presentation, which are called WordArt.

Adding WordArt

1 Click the Insert tab

2 Click on the WordArt icon from the Text group

Don't forget

You can change the size and rotation of the WordArt text box by using the handles, just as you can do with shapes.

3 Select the WordArt style that you want to use from the available options displayed

4 A WordArt text box will appear, with the words Your Text Here, click on this box to activate it

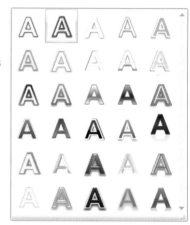

5 Replace the sample text with your own text

6 Move the text box to the correct location on the slide

Formatting WordArt

Once you have added some WordArt, you can easily apply
formatting to it, including changing the file, the outline and any
of the effects.

1 Click on the WordArt text box to display the Drawing
Tools tab

2 Select any of the options from the WordArt Styles group,
such as a new style

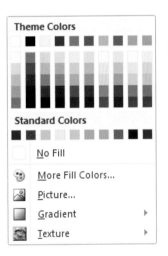

3 If you click on the down arrow
next to either Text Fill or
Text Outline, you can choose
from a number of additional
options, such as color and fill

Hot tip

Highlight the effect to
see a preview of it on
your selected text.

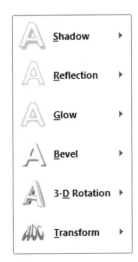

4 If you click on the down arrow
next to Text Effects, you can
choose from a number of different
text effects, such as shadow, glow
and reflection

49

5 Highlight the Text Effect you want, then choose from the available options that are displayed, depending on the effect you highlighted

6 Repeat for each WordArt text box you want to format

Formatting Text Effects

Text Effects can be easily applied to your WordArt text, which enables you to change the alignment of the text, and also the direction.

1 Click on the WordArt text box to display the Drawing Tools tab

2 Click on the Font Text Effects dialog box launcher, in the WordArt Styles group

3 Click on the Vertical alignment drop-down list to select a new alignment

4 Click on the Text direction drop-down list to change the direction of the text

5 Click Close

Find and Replace Text

There may come a time when you might need to either find a text entry in your presentation, or even replace some text with something else – for example, a person on your project may have changed and you need to update the presentation to reflect this change, so it is not out of date. Instead of having to check each and every slide in your presentation, you can use the Find function, and, if you want to replace some text, you can then use the Replace function.

1 On the Home tab, click Find from the Editing group

2 Enter the text that you want to search for in the Find what: box

51

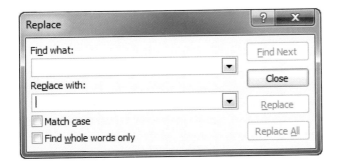

3 Click on Find Next to find the first matching entry

4 If you want to replace the entry click on Replace

5 Enter the text in the Replace with: box and click Replace

Symbols

PowerPoint 2010 comes with a large amount of different types of symbols that you can insert into your presentation. This keeps the presentation looking as professional as possible and allows you to enter freehand text for something, such as a trademark symbol.

1 Add or click on an existing text box placeholder

2 Click on the Insert tab

3 From the Symbols group, click on Symbol

4 Scroll through the list of available symbols until you find the symbol that you want to add to your slide

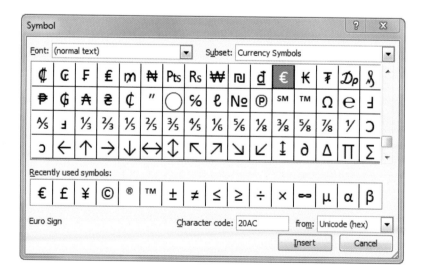

5 Click on the symbol, then click Insert to add it

Bullets and Numbers

If you want to add a list to your presentation, you might want to consider making it a bulleted or number list. PowerPoint 2010 provides a number of built-in bullet and number lists that you can easily select to make your list look more professional.

① Select the text you want to add bullets or numbers to

② Click on the Home tab, if it is not already selected

③ From the Paragraph group, select either the Bullets button or the Numbering button

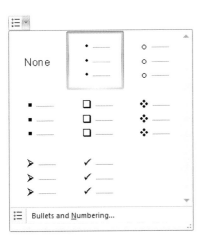

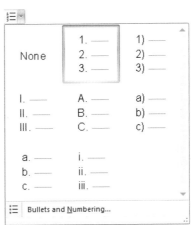

53

④ Click on the required bullet or numbering style

⑤ If you want to customize the type of bullet or number, click on Bullets and Numbering

⑥ Click the Bulleted tab, to customize Bullets

⑦ Click the Numbered tab, to customize Numbering

Editing Options

There are a number of advanced options that can be enabled, or disabled, in order to help you with the way you work with text. These options include:

- When selecting, automatically select entire word – this option will select the entire word when you select any part of the text. The default setting is enabled

- Allow text to be dragged and dropped – this option allows you to drag and drop text anywhere on the screen, or to another slide. The default setting is enabled

- Maximum number of undos – this option allows you set the maximum number of times you can use the undo button to rectify mistakes, or change what you have done. The default setting is 20 undos, and you probably won't need to change it

- Use smart cut and paste – this option is used to automatically adjust the spacing between words and objects that are pasted into the presentation. The default setting is enabled

1 Click the File tab and then click on Options

2 Click Advanced, from the left-hand column

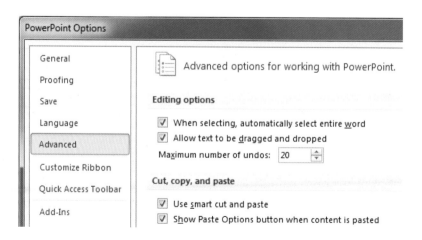

3 Check or uncheck the different settings, as required, then click OK to finish

4 Graphics and Lines

This chapter will tell you how to add various graphics, shapes, lines and arrows. It will also tell you how to edit and format what you have added. As well as looking at a new feature of PowerPoint 2010 called SmartArt.

Adding Shapes

PowerPoint 2010 comes with a number of ready-made shapes for you to use in your presentations. These shapes include rectangles, circles, arrows, lines, and many others.

1 Click on the Insert tab

2 Click on Shapes, from the Illustrations group

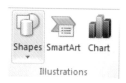

To make life even easier for you, the available shapes are grouped together by type, as well as by a top level group called Recently Used Shapes, which allows you to select a shape you have recently selected.

To draw a perfect circle or a perfect square, just hold down the Shift key after selecting the Oval or Rectangle from the shapes list.

3 Select the shape you want to add from the list of available shapes

4 You can then just point and click to the area on the slide where you want to add the shape, which will add the shape in a standard size that you can then change

5 You could also choose to hold the left mouse button down on an area of the screen and drag the box until you are happy with the size of the new shape, and, when you release the left mouse button, the shape will be drawn to that size

6 If you want to add some text to the shape, just click on the shape and type in the text you want to appear within it

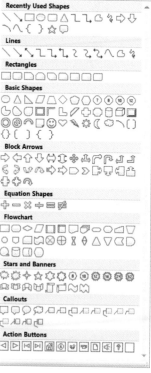

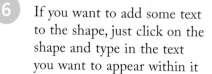

Resizing & Adjusting Shapes

You can resize or adjust any shape you have drawn, by using the various handles that will appear when a shape is selected. These handles can appear as green circles, light blue circles or yellow diamonds, depending on what their function is.

Rotation Handle (Green Circle)

Adjustment Handle (Yellow Diamond)

Sizing Handle (Light Blue Circle)

Hot tip

You might find it easier to zoom in, so that you can make precise adjustments to shapes.

Performing Adjustments or Resizing

1. Select the shape you want to resize or adjust

2. To rotate the shape, click and hold the rotation handle

3. To resize the shape, click and hold the sizing handle

4. To adjust the shape, click and hold the adjustment handle

5. Move the mouse until the shape has been resized, rotated or adjusted, as required

Hot tip

You can select any of the handles of the same type to perform the required adjustments or resizing.

Shape Effects

Another feature of PowerPoint 2010 is the ability to apply effects to shapes, such as 3-D Rotations, Shadows, Reflections, and more. You can apply quick and easy effects using any of the various preset effects, or you can select individual effects yourself.

Preset Effects

1 Select the shape you want to set the effect for

2 Click on the Format tab, if it is not already highlighted

3 From the Shapes Styles group, click on Shape Effects

4 Highlight Preset to display the Presets menu

5 Select the Preset you want to use, to apply it to the shape

6 You can also remove any preset by clicking on the No Preset option from the list

58

Individual Effects

If you did not want to use one of the preset effects, maybe because they were just not quite right, then you can choose from a large number of other effects, including:

- Shadow – the option includes effects for Outer, Inner and Perspective

- Reflection – the option is for Reflection Variations

- Glow – the option is for Glow Variations

- Soft Edges – the option includes different point size edges

- Bevel – the option is for different bevel styles

- 3-D Rotation – the option includes Parallel, Perspective and Oblique

Don't forget

If you highlight an effect, you can see a preview of it before you finalize your selection.

59

1. Select the shape you want to set the effect for

2. Click on the Format tab, if it is not already highlighted

3. From the Shape Styles group, click on Shape Effects

4. Highlight the effects style you want to select from

5. Select the effect you want to use, to apply it to the shape

| Preset ▸ |
| Shadow ▸ |
| Reflection ▸ |
| Glow ▸ |
| Soft Edges ▸ |
| Bevel ▸ |
| 3-D Rotation ▸ |

Some of the effect styles have additional Option choices, which you can select in order to make some very specific adjustments.

3-D Effects

You can add 3-D effects to any of your shapes, by either selecting from the various 3-D effects that are available, or by effectively creating your own by adjusting a number of available settings.

3-D Format Settings

These settings include:

- Bevel – gives the appearance of a raised edge and highlights the edges. You can set the width and height for the raised edge on the top or bottom of the shape

- Depth – used to show distance between the shape and its surface. You can set the color and the depth on the shape

- Contour – used to show a raised border on the whole shape. You can set the color and the size on the shape

- Surface – used to change the material look of the shape, also the level of lighting on the shape, as well as the angle of the shape. Choices include special effects, translucent effects, neutral, warm, and cool lighting

60

1. Select the shape you want to adjust and click on it

2. Click the Format tab

3. Click on Shape Effects, from the Shape Styles group

4. Click on Bevel, then click on 3-D Options

5. Make the necessary changes to the shape

6. Click Close

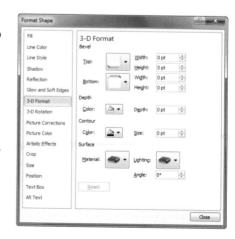

3-D Rotation Settings

These settings include:

- Presets – you can choose from the various presets, as you did previously

- Rotation – used to adjust the orientation and position of the shape, by adjusting settings for the X axis (horizontal), the Y axis (vertical) and the Z axis (height against other shapes). You can also adjust the perspective of the shape to increase or decrease the foreshortening (the depth dependent growing and shrinking). You can set the perspective between 0 and 120

- Text – used to keep the text flat and prevent it from rotating with the shape

- Object position – used to move the shape backward or forward in 3-D space

Hot tip

You can use these settings to change shapes, lines, charts and pictures as well.

1 Select the shape you want to adjust and click on it

2 Click the Format tab

3 Click on Shape Effects, from the Shape Styles group

4 Click on 3-D Rotation and select 3-D Rotation Options, from the right of the window

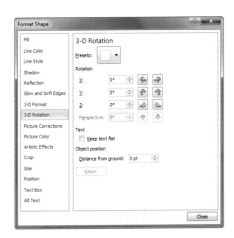

5 Make the necessary changes to the shape

6 Click Close

61

SmartArt

SmartArt was a new feature introduced with PowerPoint 2007. A SmartArt graphic allows you to easily show your information or data, without having to create a complex diagram from scratch. Once you have created a SmartArt graphic, it is very easy to modify the content, the look, and the feel.

There are a number of built-in SmartArt graphics to get you started, including lists, processes, hierachies and relationships. Choosing the right one will depend on what you are trying to show with the graphic, you could select Hierarchy if you wanted to create an organizational chart for example.

You can choose a SmartArt graphic and enter your text, or you can convert some of your existing text into a SmartArt graphic.

Create a SmartArt Graphic

1 Click on the Insert tab and select the SmartArt button, from the Illustrations group

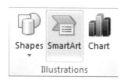

2 Choose the category and then the style of the graphic

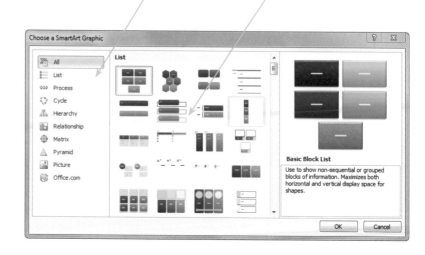

Type	Use
List	Shows non-sequential information
Process	Shows steps in a process or timeline
Cycle	Shows a continual process
Hierarchy	Used to create an organizational chart or decision tree
Relationship	Illustrates connections
Matrix	Shows how parts relate to a whole
Pyramid	Shows proportional relationships, with the largest component on top or bottom

3 Look at the preview to make sure you are happy with your selection, then click OK

4 Enter the text in the relevant [Text] boxes to see it displayed in your chosen graphic

5 Click outside of the graphic to finish

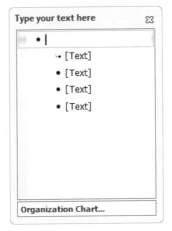

Hot tip

If the text entry box is not displayed, click on the tab with the arrows to the left of the SmartArt graphic image.

63

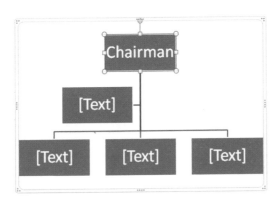

Modifying SmartArt

Now that you have created your SmartArt graphic, you can modify it to suit your presentation. These modifications can include changing the layout, the style, the color, and more, as you need.

Changing the Layout

You can easily select a different layout by selecting one from the group of Layouts that are available to you.

1 Select the SmartArt graphic you want to change

2 Ensure the Design tab is active, under SmartArt Tools

3 In the Layouts box, select the new layout, or click on the More arrow button to show additional layouts

Layouts

Changing the Style

You can easily select a different style by selecting one from the group of Quick Styles that are available to you.

1 Select the SmartArt graphic you want to change

2 Ensure the Design tab is active, under SmartArt Tools

3 In the SmartArt Styles box, select the new style, or click on the More arrow button to show additional styles

SmartArt Styles

4 If you want to change the color variation applied to the SmartArt graphic, click on the Change Colors button

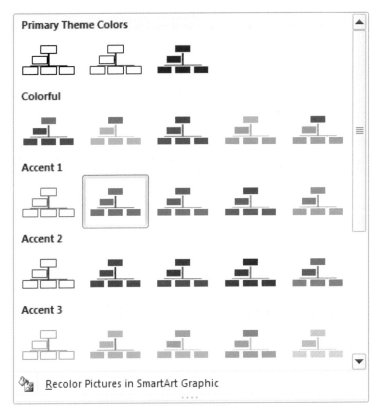

Don't forget

When you select an existing SmartArt graphic, both the current layout and style are highlighted in an orange border, to make it easy to see.

5 Scroll through the list of colors and select the one that matches your requirement

Resetting a SmartArt Graphic

If you make a mistake, or you change your mind, it is very easy to reset the graphic back to its original look before the change.

1 From the Design tab click the Reset button

Converting to SmartArt

You don't have to create the SmartArt graphic then enter your text. If you already have some text on a slide, you can easily convert it to a SmartArt graphic with the click of the mouse.

1 Select the text placeholder on the slide that you want to convert to a SmartArt graphic, so that it is highlighted

2 Click the Convert to SmartArt icon from the Paragraph group on the Home tab

3 Select the SmartArt graphic layout that you want to use for your slide (you can also click the More SmartArt Graphics button to see more)

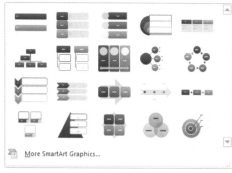

Don't forget

If you are not happy with the way the SmartArt graphic appears, you can either change it, or press the Undo button on the Quick Access Toolbar to revert the text back to its original state.

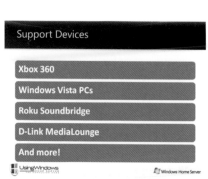

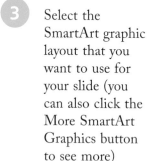

4 Check that you are happy with the layout

5 Repeat the steps for all the text that you want to convert into SmartArt graphics

Ruler and Gridlines

To make the positioning of placeholders and other objects easier, you can display a ruler and gridlines.

1 Click on the View tab

2 From the Show/Hide group click Ruler to display the Ruler, and click Gridlines to display Gridlines

☐ Ruler
☐ Gridlines
☐ Guides
Show ⤢

The Slide Pane with the Ruler Displayed

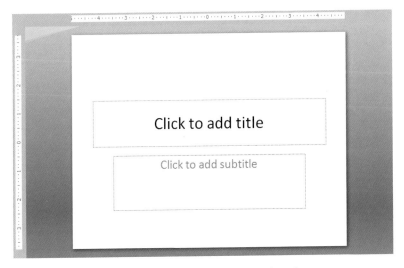

Click to add title

Click to add subtitle

The Slide Pane with Gridlines Displayed

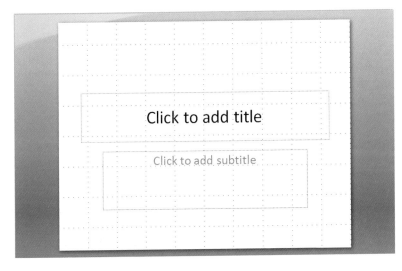

Click to add title

Click to add subtitle

67

Hot tip

You can display both the Ruler and the Gridlines at the same time, if you need to.

Hot tip

Only switch on the Gridlines when you need to, switch them off again when you have performed the action you need, to reduce the clutter on the screen.

Arrangements

There might come a time when you want to change the arrangements of either your shapes, pictures, text or other objects within your presentations. These arrangement changes could be changing the position, rotating or flipping them, or changing the order of a group of objects.

Rotating and Flipping Objects

1 Select the object you want to rotate or flip

2 Click on the Format tab

3 Click on Rotate, from the Arrange group

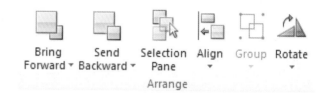

4 Click on Rotate to rotate the object either 90 degrees left or right

5 Click on Flip to flip the object vertically or horizontally

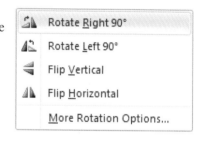

Changing Object Sizes

You can change the size of an object in many different ways. One of the quickest ways is to alter the figures in the Size group.

1 Click on the object you want to resize, then click the Format tab

2 Enter the new Height and Width in the Size group

Height: 2.8 cm

Width: 8 cm

Size

Changing Object Position

You can change the position of any object, for example, bringing it forward or moving it back in comparison to any other object.

1 Select the object you want to change the position of

2 Click on the Format tab

3 Select Bring to Front, from the Arrange group

Selection Pane

Sometimes it would be easier to work on a slide if some of the objects were not there. You can easily hide and then show any object on a slide, making it easier for you to work on and even layer objects into your presentation.

1 Click on any object on the slide

2 Click on the Format tab

3 Click on Selection Pane, from the Arrange group

4 Click on any listed object to highlight it on the slide

5 If you want to hide the object, click on the Eye icon

6 To show the hidden object again, click on the Eye icon once more

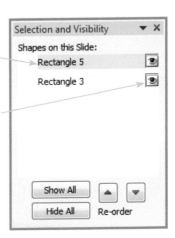

Hot tip

You should consider using the selection pane if some of the objects on the slide are not easily accessible.

Lines and Arrows

Most presentations will, at some point, include a line or an arrow. It is very easy to add a simple line and then format it to suit your purposes, which can also include adding arrow heads to the line.

Hot tip

When you start the line drawing process, it really doesn't matter whether you select Shapes from the Home tab or the Insert tab.

Drawing a Line

1 Click on the Home tab or the Insert tab

2 Click the Shapes button, in the Drawing group

3 Select a Line or Arrow shape from the available list

Lines

4 Click and drag the mouse pointer to add the line to your presentation (you can make the line as long as you want and, at whichever angle you want as well)

5 Release the mouse button to draw the line

Hot tip

You can use the handles on the end of the line to change the size or orientation.

Adding a Quick Style to a Line

1 Click on the line that you want to add the Quick Style to

2 Click on the Home tab

3 Click on the Quick Styles button, from the Drawing group

Quick Styles ▾

4 Highlight the style you want to use, and check that it looks OK on your slide

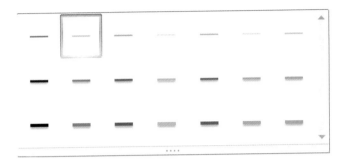

5 If you are happy with the way the new style looks, click on the style to make the change

6 Repeat the steps for each line you want to add a Quick Style to

Adding Arrows to Lines

1 Click on the line that you want to add an arrow to

2 Click on the Format tab

3 Click on the Shape Outline button, from the Shape Styles group

4 Click on the Arrows button

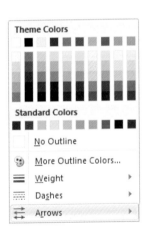

Hot tip

You can see a preview of the arrow by hovering over the selection.

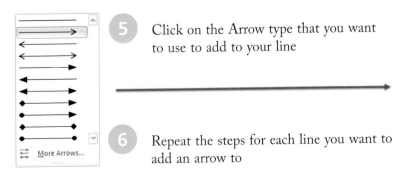

5 Click on the Arrow type that you want to use to add to your line

6 Repeat the steps for each line you want to add an arrow to

...cont'd

Modifying a Line

1 Click on the Line that you want to modify, then click on the Format tab

2 Click on the Shape Outline button, from the Shape Styles group

3 To change the thickness of the line, click on Weight

4 Choose the thickness you want to apply to your line

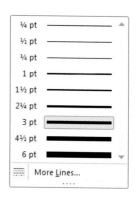

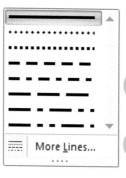

5 To change the style of the line, click on Dashes

6 Choose the style you want to apply to your line

Formatting a Line

You can also make formatting changes to the lines.

1 Select the line you want to format, then click the Format tab

2 Click the Format Shape dialog box launcher, from the Shape Styles group

3 Adjust the various settings as required and click Close

Hot tip

You can change a number of the parameters for lines from the Format Shape dialog box, including line width, dash type, arrow settings, and much more.

Freeforms and Scribbles

Within the available choices in the Lines box, there are two additional choices – Freeform and Scribble. Both can be used to create customized lines or shapes. You would use Freeform if you wanted to create a shape that has both curved and straight segments, and you would use Scribble if you wanted to create a line or shape that looked like it had been drawn by hand with a pen.

Freeforms – Straight Lines

1 Click on the Home or Insert tab

2 Click on Shapes, then select the Freeform icon from Lines

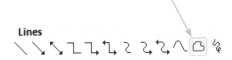

3 Click the location on the slide where you want to start the freeform

4 If you want to draw straight lines, keep moving the mouse pointer, and press the left mouse button each time you want to change direction

5 Either double-click the mouse button to stop drawing, or press the ESC key on your keyboard

Freeforms – Curves

1 To draw curves, just repeat steps 1 through 3 above, only this time, hold down the mouse button and drag the mouse to draw

Hot tip

Once you have drawn the line or shape, you can easily change the weight, color and other properties, by selecting what you want to change and clicking on the Format tab.

2 Release the mouse button when you have finished

Freeforms – Filled Shapes

1 To draw a filled shape, repeat steps 1 through 3 from the Straight Lines section

2 Using a combination of holding the mouse button down to draw straight lines and releasing the mouse button to draw curves, draw the shape you want to appear

3 To complete the shape, and fill it in automatically, you must join the last point to the first point

Scribbles

1 Click on the Home or Insert tab

2 Click on Shapes and select the Scribble icon from Lines

Don't forget

You can also create a filled scribble, by joining up the start and end points of the scribble, just as you did for a filled freeform shape.

Lines

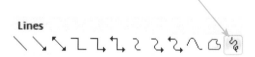

3 Click and hold the mouse button on the start point

4 Drag the mouse pointer across the slide, drawing your shape

5 Release the mouse button

74

5 Tables and Charts

This chapter will explain some of the table and chart options provided by PowerPoint 2010, including the ability to use Excel 2010 functionality.

Tables

Tables have been greatly enhanced in PowerPoint 2010, for example, it is now much easier to reuse a table that you already have in Word 2010 or Excel 2010.

Adding a Table

There are a number of ways to add a table to your presentation.

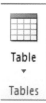

Table
▾
Tables

1 Click the Insert tab on the toolbar

2 Click Table

76

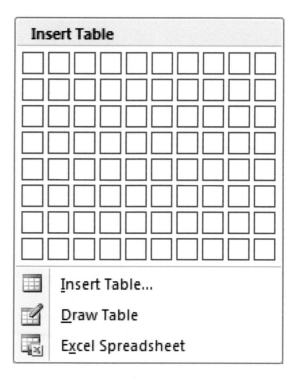

3 Highlight the number of rows and columns that you want to represent your table (such as 2 down and 5 across), then click the mouse button to add the table to the slide

That is not the only way to add a new table into your presentation, there are some others that you could use.

Inserting a Table

1 Click the Insert tab on the toolbar

2 Click Table

3 Click Insert Table, from the bottom of the Insert Table section

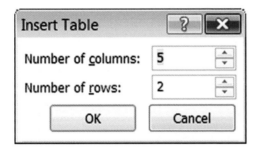

Hot tip

To add an additional row at the end of your table, click on the last cell in the last row and press the TAB button on your keyboard.

4 Enter the number of required columns and rows for the table

5 Click OK to add the table to the slide

Inserting a Table on a New Slide

There is also another way of adding a new table to a slide. If you are creating a new slide, and the slide layout includes a set of icons for adding either tables, charts, graphics and others, you can simply click on the table icon to launch the Insert Table dialog box.

Table Styles and Layouts

Once you have created your table, you can apply different styles to it, change the borders, change the colors and more.

Table styles are a combination of different formatting options, including colors, which are determined by the theme colors of your presentation. To change the style:

Hot tip

After you have made the changes to the table style, you can set the style as the default by right-clicking the table style and selecting Set as Default.

1 Select the table you want to change styles for

2 Under Table Tools, on the Design tab, choose a style from the thumbnailed Table Styles group

Table Styles

78

3 Click on Table Effects to add an effect, such as a shadow or reflection

Cell Bevel ▶

Shadow ▶

Reflection ▶

Don't forget

The Reflection or Shadow effect can only be applied to an entire table.

4 Click on Shading to change either the theme colors or the standard colors

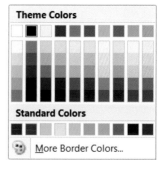

Theme Colors

Standard Colors

More Border Colors...

5 If you only want to change a specific part of the table, use the Table Style Options group

☑ Header Row   ☐ First Column

☐ Total Row   ☐ Last Column

☑ Banded Rows ☐ Banded Columns

Table Style Options

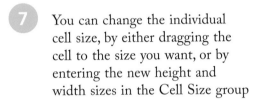

6 Click on the Borders button to bring up the various border options you can change, for example, adding or removing borders from certain cells

7 You can change the individual cell size, by either dragging the cell to the size you want, or by entering the new height and width sizes in the Cell Size group

Cell Size

Rows and Columns

If you need to, you can add or remove rows and columns, or even merge cells together, or split cells up.

1 Click on the cell above or below the row you want to add, or to the left or right of a column

2 Click on the Layout tab, under Table Tools, go to the Rows & Columns group

Rows & Columns

3 Click on the button that represents what and where you want to add, for example, click Insert Above if you want the row to be added above your current cell position

Drawing a Table

You an also add a table by drawing its borders and changing its design and layout by hand.

1 Click the Insert tab on the toolbar

2 Click Table

3 Click Draw Table, from the bottom of the Insert Table section

4 The pointer will change into a pencil, you can then click and drag a box to the size you want the table to be, in order to draw the border of a table. You can also continue to draw lines with the pencil within the border, to add columns and rows

5 If you make a mistake and add a line, you can easily remove it by selecting the Eraser. This changes the pointer to an eraser and you only have to click on a line to remove it

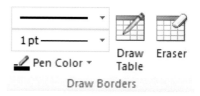

1 pt

Pen Color ▾ Draw Table Eraser

Draw Borders

6 You can also change the border type, the line thickness, and the color of the pen used, from this group

7 If you need to change the size of the table, enter the new height and width in the Table Size group

Height: 6.18 cm

Width: 16.93 cm

Lock Aspect Ratio

Table Size

Hot tip

If you hold down the SHIFT button while the pointer is a pencil, it will act like an eraser.

Hot tip

You can also use the eraser to merge cells, by double-clicking on the cell borders you want to remove.

Hot tip

If you want to keep the same ratio between the height and width when you resize your table, check the Lock Aspect Ratio box on the Table Size group.

Chart Types

PowerPoint 2010 supports a large number of different types of charts, including pie charts, bar charts, line charts, and many more.

The following is a very brief description of some of the available chart types, to help you decide which might be the right one for your presentation:

Column
Column charts are useful for showing changes in data over periods of time, and are useful for showing comparisons between data.

Line
Line charts are useful for displaying data over periods of time, and display trends in that data.

Pie
Pie charts show the data as a percentage of the whole in segments, and are used to display statistics.

Bar
Bar charts use vertical or horizontal bars to show comparisons among two or more items.

Area
Each area is given a solid color or pattern, to emphasize the relationships between the pieces of charted information.

Stock
This chart is useful if you want to easily display stock prices.

Doughnut
This chart is very similar to a pie chart, but contains more than one data series.

Radar
Radar charts are used to compare the aggregate values of a number of data series.

Hot tip

Each chart type has a number of different subtypes available to select from, including 3-D charts.

Hot tip

For more detailed descriptions of all the available chart types, including examples, check out the Help function in PowerPoint and search for available chart types.

Adding Charts

Once you have decided on what type of chart you want to use, adding it to your presentation is very simple.

1 Click on the Insert tab

2 From the Illustrations group, click on Chart

3 Click on the chart type you want to use

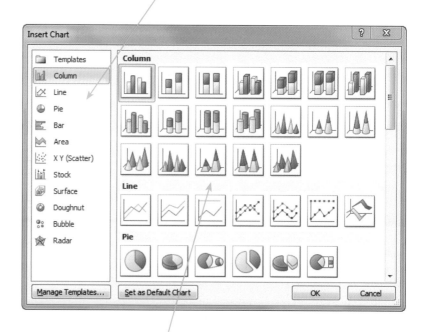

4 Click on the chart subtype you want to use

5 Click OK to create the new chart

6 Enter the data you want, and change any of the data labels that appear in the sample

	A	B
1	Column1	Emails Sent
2	1st Qtr	45
3	2nd Qtr	28
4	3rd Qtr	79
5	4th Qtr	34

Hot tip

If you have Excel 2010, make sure it is installed so that PowerPoint 2010 uses this for data entry and manipulation. If you don't have Excel, Microsoft Graph is used instead.

7 Close Excel, your chart will be updated in PowerPoint

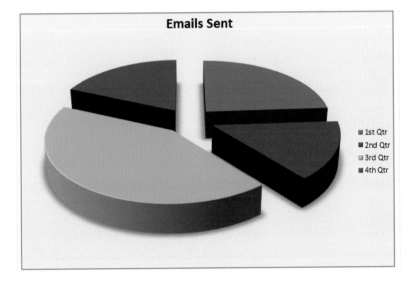

Emails Sent

- 1st Qtr
- 2nd Qtr
- 3rd Qtr
- 4th Qtr

Don't forget

If you want to use the data again, make sure you save the Excel worksheet.

8 If you want to use a different type of chart, you can easily change it by clicking on the Change Chart Type button in the type group and selecting a different chart type

Change Chart Type   Save As Template

Type

9 Add any text or graphics you want to use with the chart

83

Enhancing the Charts

You can do a lot to enhance the look of your charts. This section will give you an introduction to what is available in PowerPoint.

Chart Styles

There are numerous different styles you can choose from for your chart, ranging from standard flat charts to full color 3-D charts.

1 Highlight the chart you want to enhance and, on the Chart Styles menu, choose a new style from the ones available

Chart Styles

2 Click on your chosen style and your chart will automatically be updated to reflect the new style

Adding Labels and Titles

Now that your chart has been created, you can add a legend and any other labels you need, to make the meaning of the chart as clear as possible.

1 Click on the Layout tab, under the Chart Tools title and on the Labels group, click on the option you want to add, for example, Chart Title

Chart Title ▾ Axis Titles ▾ Legend ▾ Data Labels ▾ Data Table ▾

Labels

2 Choose the title option you want to use and enter the title for the chart

Axes and Gridlines

Depending on your chart type, you can display or hide both axes and gridlines.

1 Click on the Layout tab, under the Chart Tools title

2 On the Axes group, click either the Axes button or the Gridlines button and make a selection from the available options. For example, if you want to display an axis, click on the type of axis you want to display and then choose one of the options

Axes   Gridlines

Axes

Don't forget

You cannot use all the enhancements on every type of chart – if the option is not highlighted you cannot use it.

Changing the Format of Elements

You can change the format of individual elements of your chart, or the whole chart itself.

1 Click on the Format tab, under the Chart Tools title

2 On the Current Selection group, click on the arrow to choose the element you want to select

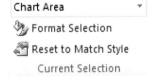

Chart Area

Format Selection

Reset to Match Style

Current Selection

3 Click on Format Selection

4 Make any changes you want, if you make a mistake, or want to go back, click the Reset to Match Style button

Changing or Showing the Data

If you should decide to change the data at any time, or you want to show the data, you can by choosing the relevant option from the Data group.

1 Click on the required icon from the Data tab, to see or edit the source data

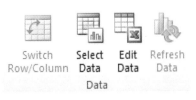

Switch Row/Column   Select Data   Edit Data   Refresh Data

Data

Using Excel 2010

Excel Charts

When you copy a chart that you have created in Excel 2010, and paste it into PowerPoint 2010, the chart data is then linked with the Excel worksheet. If you want to update the data at anytime, you must update the Excel worksheet, which, in turn, updates the chart in PowerPoint.

1. In Excel, make sure you have already created the chart, then select the chart by clicking the border and selecting Copy from the Clipboard group

2. Go to your PowerPoint presentation

3. Click on Paste, from the Clipboard group, to paste the Excel chart onto your slide

Copying Excel Tables

You can easily create a new Excel table in PowerPoint, or you can copy and paste an existing table directly from Excel.

1. In Excel, make sure you have already created the table, then select the table by clicking the border and selecting Copy from the Clipboard group

2. Go to your PowerPoint presentation

3. Click on Paste, from the Clipboard group, to paste the Excel table onto your slide

Inserting Excel Tables

If you have not yet created your table in Excel, you can create it directly in PowerPoint.

1. Click the Insert tab on the toolbar and click Table

2. Click on Excel Spreadsheet to add a blank Excel table

6 Enhancing Presentations

This chapter will tell you how to enhance your presentation, using very simple but effective options.

Themes

If you want to give your presentation a professional look and feel, without having to spend a considerable amount of time formatting it, you could use one of PowerPoint's many themes.

A theme includes specific colors, fonts, and effects.

You can even create your own themes, if there is not one that suits your needs, and you can then reuse it later.

Applying a Theme

1 Click on the Design tab

2 In the Themes group, click on the More button to reveal all of the available themes

3 Click on the theme that you want to use

As you can see from the examples below, just by selecting a different theme, your presentation can be dramatically different.

Themes can be applied to an entire presentation or to individual slides, the choice is entirely yours. You can even set a theme to be the default. Right-click the theme for these options.

Effects

Theme effects are collections of lines and fills that are part of each theme. Unlike colors and fonts, you cannot create your own effects, however, you can select which effect you want to use in your theme.

1 In the Themes group, click on the Effects button to display the effects list

2 Scroll through the effects list and click on the effect you wish to use for your theme

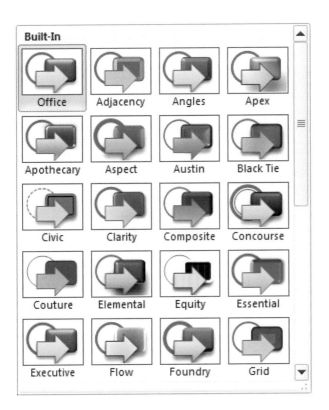

As you can see, each effect is slightly different, so it may be a case of trial and error, choosing between them until you find one that suits your presentation.

Customizing Themes

You can change the colors, the fonts, and the line and fill effects that are used for a specific theme. You can then immediately use that changed theme, or save it as a custom theme so that you can use it again later, in a different presentation.

Theme Colors

Each theme contains four text and background colors, six accent colors, and two hyperlink colors. The four colors in the square buttons are the current text and background colors, the eight colored squares that appear in the color list represent the accent colors and hyperlink colors, in that order.

Don't forget

You can easily use one of the existing color schemes by selecting it from the theme colors list.

90

1. In the Themes group, click on the Colors button to display the colors list

2. Scroll through the colors list and click on the Create New Theme Colors button

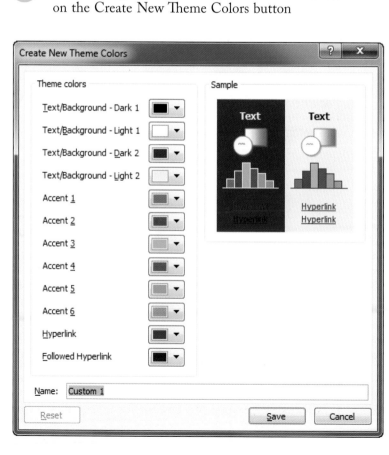

3 Click on the boxes next to each color option, and select the new color you want to use for that option

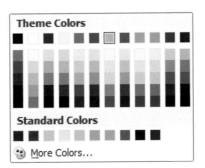

4 Enter a name for your new custom theme, then click Save

Don't forget

If you want to reset the theme colors back to their original settings, click on the Reset button before you click Save.

Theme Fonts

Each theme font contains a heading and a body font, and these can both be different fonts if you wish.

1 In the Themes group, click on the Fonts button to display the colors list

2 Scroll through the colors list and click on the Create New Theme Fonts button

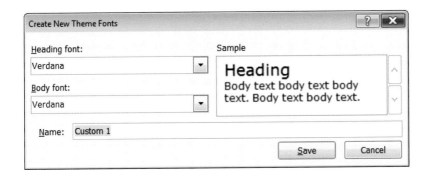

Hot tip

Save your new theme so that you can apply it to any other presentation in the future. Click on the More button and then click Save Current Theme.

3 Select the fonts you want to use for both the Heading and the Body

4 Enter a name for your new custom font, then click Save

91

Animations

You can add animations to a number of different elements in your presentation, including text, sounds, graphics, SmartArt diagrams, and more. This can help to greatly enhance the presentation, and is quick and easy to do, leaving you more time to concentrate on the content.

You can use one of the built-in animations, or you can create your own, and you can apply the animations to the whole slide or to different elements, so each element could have a different effect.

The animations also have specific effects associated with them.

You can also add slide transitions to enhance the effect even more. We will cover slide transitions later.

Beware

Even though you can apply a different animation to any part of the slide, try not to use too many, as it can detract from the presentation rather than enhance it!

Hot tip

To remove an animation, select the animated object and click on No Animation, from the Animate list.

1 Highlight the word, letter, or whatever object you want to animate

2 Click on the Animations tab and, in the Animations group, click on the Animation Styles button

3 Choose the effect from the list of available options, you will then be shown a short preview of what the animation will look like

4 Choose any other objects you want to add effects to and repeat the above steps

5 If you want to then see what the whole thing looks like, click the Preview button

Advanced Animations

You use custom animations when you want to control exactly what happens and when.

1 Highlight the word, letter, or whatever object you want to animate

2 Click on the Animations tab and, in the Advanced Animations group, click on the Add Animation button

Hot tip

You can view your entire presentation by clicking the Slide Show button at the bottom of the Custom Animation box.

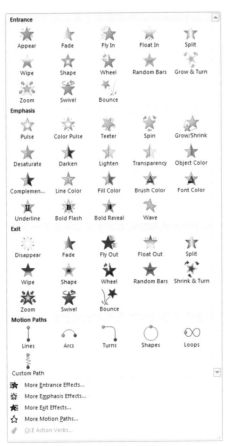

3 Click on the type of effect you want to add, for example, Motion Paths if you want to create your own path for the object

4 Choose the path you want to use, or click highlight Custom Path

Hot tip

You can choose from other available options by clicking on one of the More buttons.

5 Click on the start point with your mouse and move around the screen, clicking on each point, press Enter when you are finished to see a preview of the animation

...cont'd

Each effect you add will be numbered, and you can see the start point, path and end point for each effect by the number appearing on the slide.

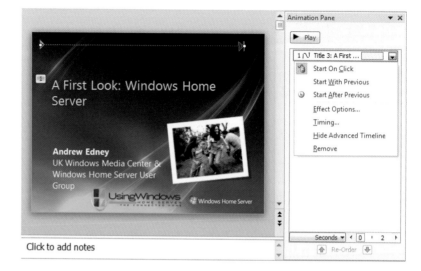

 For each animation, you can select how it starts, its path, and the speed it will go from the Timing menu

You can even add sound to the animation, by clicking the animation in the list and selecting Effect Options

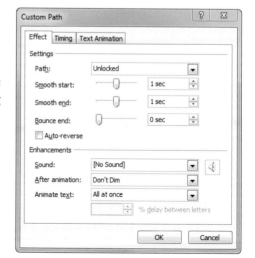

Make any changes you want to the Effect, the Timing, and the Text Animation

Animating SmartArt

You can add animations to your SmartArt graphics, or to individual shapes in your SmartArt graphic.

As with other animations, the actual animations available will depend on the layout you selected for your SmartArt graphic. The animations you can apply to SmartArt graphics are different from the animations that you may have applied to other objects.

These differences include:

- The connecting lines between each of the shapes are always associated with the second shape, and are not animated individually

- Animations will appear in the order that the shapes in the SmartArt graphics appear. You can reverse the order but you cannot change the sequence, unless you create multiple slides

1 Highlight the SmartArt graphic you want to animate

2 Click on the Animations tab and, in the Animations group, click on the animation you want to use

You can also add animation effects. The available animation effects you can use include:

- As one object – the SmartArt graphic is treated as though it was a single object, rather than multiple objects

- All at once – all the shapes in the SmartArt graphic are animated simultaneously. This is different to the As one object animation, where the entire object is animated as a single object

- One by one – each shape is animated one at a time

- Level at once – all the shapes in the same branch are animated at the same time

- Level one by one – all the shapes are animated first by level, and then individually within the level

Beware

Even though you can apply a different animation to any part of the SmartArt graphic, try not to use too many, as it can detract from the presentation rather than enhance it!

Beware

Beware when running a Macro – make sure you know what it is doing and where it is from. See the Security chapter later in the book for more information on Macros.

Hot tip

You can also add an action to an existing object, or piece of text, highlighting it and clicking on the Action button in the Links group.

Hot tip

Use the Custom action button to define your own shape – you can pretty much make it look like anything you want.

Actions

An action button can be used in your presentation to perform a function, such as linking to something, or even running a separate program or macro.

Action buttons can be predefined buttons, shapes and arrows – for example, if you wanted an action button to be used to move to the next slide in a self-running presentation, you could use a right arrow to perform this function for you.

Adding an Action Button

You can add action buttons that activate the action when they are clicked, or even when they have the mouse go over them.

1 Click the Insert tab and click on the More arrow in the Shapes Group

2 Scroll down to the Action Buttons group of icons

Action Buttons

There are a number of predefined action buttons you can select from, including forward and back, information, movie, sound, or even custom. These buttons do not have any actions associated with them, but they are useful if you don't want to have to create something new.

3 Click on the action button you want to add

4 Click and drag to add the action button onto the slide and launch the Action Settings dialog box

5 If you want the action to be performed when you click the button, ensure the Mouse Click tab is active. If you want the action to be performed when the pointer moves over the button, click on the Mouse Over tab

Action Settings

| Mouse Click | Mouse Over |

Action on click

- ⦿ None
- ○ Hyperlink to:
  - Next Slide ▾
- ○ Run program:
  - [_____] Browse...
- ○ Run macro:
  - [_____] ▾
- ○ Object action:
  - [_____] ▾

- ☐ Play sound:
  - [No Sound] ▾
- ☐ Highlight click

OK   Cancel

Don't forget

The Macro and Object settings are only available if your presentation contains either a macro or an OLE object.

6 Click on the button that represents the action you want performed, for example, if you want to link to another slide, click the Hyperlink to button

7 Choose the slide to link to, or browse for the program to run, if that was what you selected

8 Click OK

Hot tip

Add sounds to the action to enhance the presentation.

The action button will then appear on the screen, you can then change the size and shape, or add text to it, by double-clicking on the button and choosing from the format options.

Hyperlinks

A hyperlink is used to link a piece of text or object, such as a picture, another slide in the presentation, a slide in a different presentation, a file, a web page, or even an email address, depending on what you need the link for.

Link to Another Slide in Your Presentation

1. Select the text or the object you want to use as the link

2. Click on the Insert tab, then click on the Hyperlink button in the Links group to launch the Edit Hyperlink dialog box

98

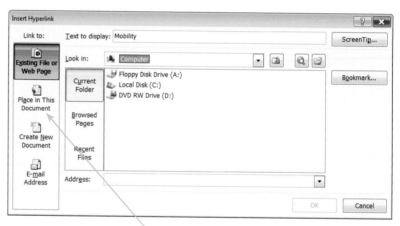

3. Click on the Place in This Document button, then choose the slide from the list of available slides to go to when the link is clicked, then click OK to finish

4. If you choose a piece of text it will appear with a line underneath it. Click the text to activate the link

5. You can edit, open, copy or remove the link by right-clicking on the link

Edit Hyperlink...

Open Hyperlink

Copy Hyperlink

Remove Hyperlink

Create a Link to an E-mail Address

1 Click on the E-mail Address button from the Edit Hyperlink dialog box

2 Enter the e-mail address you want to send to, and also enter a Subject for the message, and then click OK

Link to a Slide in a Different Presentation

You can even link to a slide that can be found in a completely different presentation.

1 Click on the Existing File or Web Page button, from the Edit Hyperlink dialog box

2 Click on the presentation you want to use the slide from

3 Click on the Bookmark button

4 Scroll through the list of slides in the presentation you have selected, click on the one you want to link to

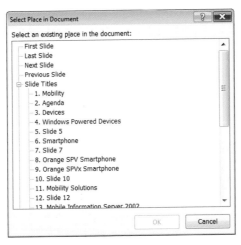

5 Click OK

Don't forget

If you create a link to something, and you later move that something, make sure you update the link or it won't work!

Headers and Footers

Headers and Footers are there to enable you to add information to your slides, handouts and notes. This information can include:

- The date and/or time
- The slide number
- Titles, for example, the title of the presentation
- And much more

Adding a Footer to a Slide

Hot tip

Slides, by default, do not contain headers, however, you can move a footer to be a header quite easily.

1 Click on the Insert tab

2 Click the Header and Footer icon from the Text group

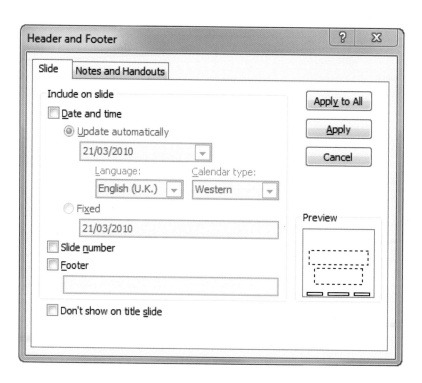

Hot tip

When you check something to include on the slide, the preview window will highlight where the item will be displayed on the slide.

3 Check the Footer box and enter the text you want

4 Click Apply for that slide, or Apply to All for all slides

5 If you want to add the date and time, or the slide number to the slides, check the relevant boxes

Adding Headers and Footers to Handouts & Notes

1 Click on the Insert tab

2 Click the Header and Footer icon from the Text group

3 Click on the Notes and Handouts tab

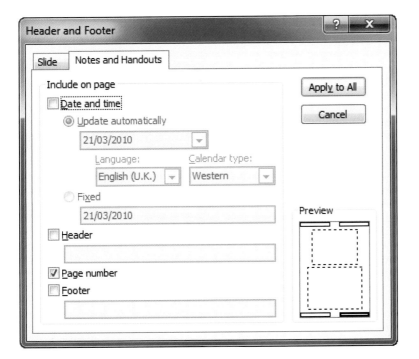

4 Check the boxes for what you want to include

5 If you want to add the date and time, or the slide number to the slides, check the relevant boxes

6 Click Apply to All

Background Styles

Background styles are used, along with the themes and effects, to make your presentation look just that little bit more professional. A background style is created from a combination of theme colors and the currently selected document theme.

Add a Background Style

1 Click on the Design tab

2 Click on the Background Styles button, from the Background group, to display a list of available styles

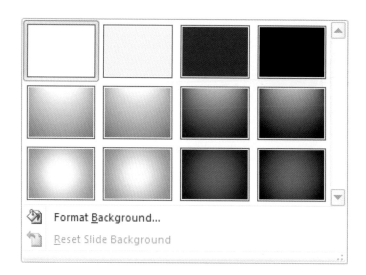

3 When you have decided on which style to choose, right-click and then click Apply to Selected Slides (if you have selected individual slides to change), or click on Apply to All Slides to have the new style applied throughout your presentation

You can also customize a background style by clicking on the Format Background button and then changing the options to suit the background, as you see fit.

Hot tip

In earlier versions of PowerPoint, you needed a design template to set a background. In PowerPoint 2010 you add a background style.

Hot tip

Hover over the background style to preview your slides with that style.

Hot tip

Make your presentation handouts easier to read by hiding background objects. To do this, place a check in the Hide Background Graphics box in the Background group.

7 Multimedia Experience

This chapter will tell you about the different multimedia options available in PowerPoint, and how to use them to your advantage.

Adding Videos

Videos can be used to enhance your presentation and can be added from either files on your computer, or from the clip organizer (which will be covered later in this chapter).

Adding videos from files on your computer

1 Go to the slide where you want to add the video, or videos

2 Click on the Insert tab and click on the arrow under Video from the Media menu

Video Audio
Media

Don't forget

You can only add videos that have a supported format. If you are not sure if your video is supported, you can check the Media Formats page later in this chapter.

3 Click on Video from File

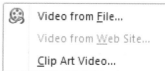
Video from File...
Video from Web Site...
Clip Art Video...

4 Select the Video you want to add

A still image of the start of the video will then appear on the slide, taking up most, if not all, of the slide space.

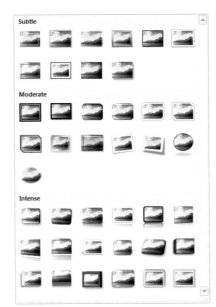

5 Change the size of the video box, and the location of the box where appropriate, by using the various handles around the video

6 You can change the style of the video by clicking on one of the available styles, from the Video Styles menu

Adjusting the video and making corrections

Now that the video you want to use in your presentation is on the correct slide, and is sized and styled how you you want it, you can make some additional adjustments, including adjusting the brightness, contrast, and color settings.

Hot tip

If you make a number of changes to the video, and you later change your mind, you can click on the Reset Design button from the Adjust group.

1 Click on the video you want to adjust

2 Click on the required adjustment option from the Adjust menu

3 Make your selections

4 Repeat the process for each adjustment you need to make

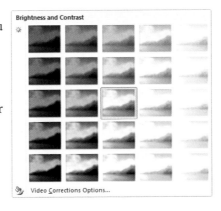

Video Options

Once you have placed the vidoeo onto a slide in your presentation, you have a number of options available to you.

The options include:

● Changing the volume

● When to play the video

● Playing the video full screen

1 Click the video you want to change the options for, to activate the Video Options menu

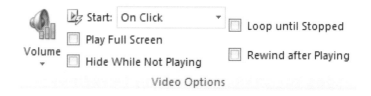

2 Change any of the settings as required, for example, if you want to play the video when it is clicked, choose On Click from the Start dialog box

Arrangements

You can easily change the arrangement of the video file on your slide, for example, by rotating it or changing its position relative to the other items on the slide (such as behind or in front of something else).

1 Click the video you want to activate the Arrange menu for

2 Select whichever arrangement option you want to use

Size and Position

You may not want to play the video full screen during your presentation, so you have the option to resize it.

1 Click the video you want to change the size of, and either adjust the height and the width to whatever size you want, or, to have more options, click on the arrow to launch the Size and Position dialog box

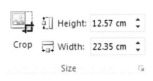

When you resize a video, the aspect ratio may change and the video may appear squashed or out of shape. To keep the aspect ratio the same, select the Lock aspect ratio check box.

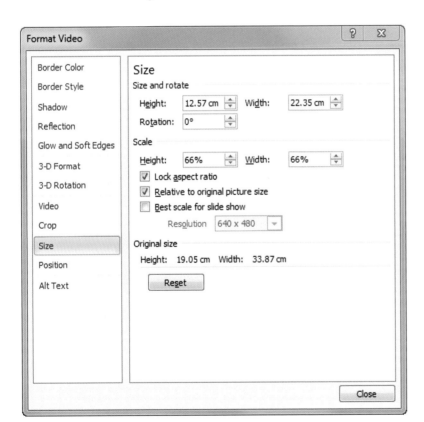

Hot tip

You can have PowerPoint scale the video file for you, to fit the resolution of the presentation, by using the Best scale for slide show check box and selecting your resolution. This will also help to prevent the video from skipping if it is sized incorrectly.

107

Don't forget

If you make a mistake, just click on the Reset button.

2 Make any changes you want to make

3 Click on Close

Trimming Video

When you add a video to your presentation, you may not want to play the whole thing. In earlier versions of PowerPoint, if you wanted to only play a part of the video, you either had to manually select the part you wanted to play or you had to edit the video before adding it to your presentation. With PowerPoint 2010, you can trim the video from within the presentation, meaning that you can choose exactly what part of the video you want to play.

1 Click on the video that you want to trim

2 On the Playback tab, click on Trim Video from the Editing group

Trim
Video

3 Move the green slider to the point on the video that you want to play from

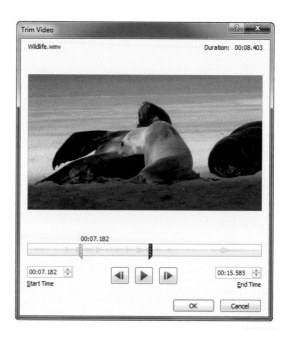

4 Move the red slider to the point on the video that you want the playback to end

5 Click OK to complete the trim

Adding Sounds

Sounds can be used to enhance your presentation, and they can be added from a number of different sources:

- From files on your computer

- From the clip organizer

- Directly from a CD

- By recording your own sounds

Adding Sounds from Files on your Computer

1 Go to the slide where you want to add the sound or sounds

Video Audio

Media

2 Click on the Insert tab and click on the arrow under Audio from the Media menu

3 Click on Audio from File

4 Select the sound you want to add

Audio from File...

Clip Art Audio...

Record Audio...

An icon that looks like a speaker will then appear on the slide. Move this icon to an appropriate position.

◀| |▶ 00:00.00 ◀))

You can preview your sound by clicking on the preview button.

▶

Play

Preview

109

Sounds from Other Sources

Playing Music from a CD

You can add music from your favorite CDs and have it play during your presentation. You can also have the music playing before or after your presentation, to give your audience something to listen to.

Don't forget

Make sure that the CD you want to play is in the drive ready to go, as the music from the CD is not actually added to your presentation.

1 Insert the CD into the CD drive of your computer

2 Select the slide you want to add the music to

3 Click on the Insert tab and then click on the arrow below the Audio button on the Media group

4 Click on Play CD Audio Track

Don't forget

If you want to use music from more than one CD, don't forget to swap the CD before you get to that slide.

Hot tip

If you want the music to play continuously, just tick the Loop until stopped button.

5   In the Clip selection area, choose your start and end track

6   Make any other selections you require, then click OK

You will be prompted for how the music will then play. You can choose between Automatically, which will play the music as soon as you go to the slide, or When Clicked, which will only play the music when you click on the CD icon.

Recording sounds

You can record your own sounds, or your voice, and add it to a slide or slides in the presentation.

1   Select the slide you want to add the sound to

2   Click on the Insert tab and then click on the arrow below the Sound button on the Media Clips group

3   Click on Record Sound and enter a name for the sound

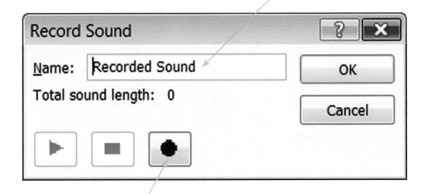

4   Click the record button to start

5   Click on the stop button when you have finished recording, then click OK to add the sound

The Clip Organizer

The Clip Organizer is a tool that sorts and organizes clips in collections for use in PowerPoint 2010, and other Microsoft Office applications.

You can use it to organize clips that are stored on your machine, or online, and even add and sort new clips.

Using the Clip Organizer

1 From the Microsoft Office 2010 Tools program files menu, click on Microsoft Clip Organizer

2 Click the Search button and enter a search

3 Or click the Collection List button and look through the available clips in the section that matches your need

4 Click on the clip that you want to use

Don't forget

Clips are photos, animations, videos, sounds, and other media files.

Hot tip

You can reduce the amount of space the catalog of clips uses on your hard disk by running the Compact tool, from the Tools menu.

Beware

Because the Clip Organizer only has pointers to the actual clips, rather than the clips themselves, if you delete the clip from your hard drive, it will no longer be available in the Clip Organizer.

5 Either press the right mouse button, or click on the down arrow that appears to the right of the selected clip

6 Click Copy

7 Go to your presentation and click Paste to insert the clip, then move it into position on the slide

Adding Collections and Clips

You can easily add your own collections and clips to the Clip Organizer.

1 Click File and highlight Add Clips to Organizer

2 Choose whether to add the clips automatically (which will search your hard disk and add everything into collections for you) or choose On My Own, which gives you the opportunity to select the clips you want to add, from any accessible location

3 Choose the clips and click Add to add them

Organizing Clips

Once the clips are in the collections list, you can perform a number of different tasks to make it easier to find them later.

These include:

- Renaming, copying, or deleting collections

- Copying or moving clips into different collections

- Adding or changing captions on clips

- Changing the properties of a collection

- Adding, modifying, or deleting keywords associated with a clip

Photo Albums

If you have ever wanted to create a photo album and deliver it as a presentation, PowerPoint 2010 makes it easy for you.

A Photo Album is a presentation that displays any photographs, along with any effects and captions you want, to make the presentation more interesting. You can even add frames around the photographs.

Creating a Photo Album

Don't forget

You can easily share your photo albums with other people, by emailing them or publishing them online.

1 Click on the Insert tab, then click on the arrow under Photo Album, from the Images menu

2 Click on New Photo Album to begin the process

Adding Photographs

Hot tip

You can easily add more than one photo at a time, by holding down the CTRL key on your keyboard while selecting additional photos.

1 Click on Insert picture from File/Disk button and choose the photographs you want to add

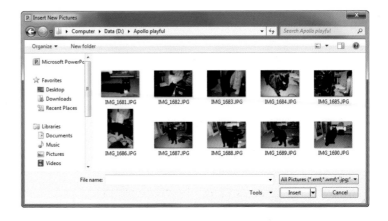

Editing the Album

Once you have added some photographs to the album, you can change the sequence they appear in, add captions, add text boxes, and more.

1 Highlight a picture in the album and use the up and down arrows to change the sequence, where necessary

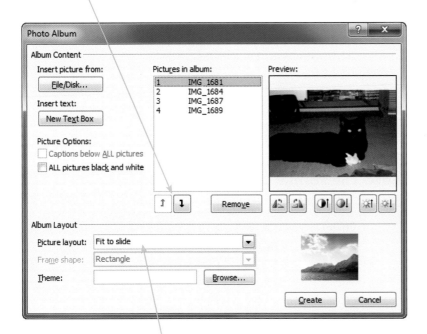

Don't forget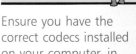

Ensure you have the correct codecs installed on your computer, in order to play back some of the formats listed.

2 Change the picture layout to whatever you want

Changing the Photograph Appearance

1 Select a picture in the album

- To rotate a picture, use
- To change the contrast, use
- To change the brightness, use

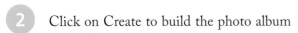

2 Click on Create to build the photo album

Media Formats

PowerPoint 2010 supports a number of different audio and video file formats, including:

Audio File Formats

File Format	Description
.aiff	Audio Interchange File Format
.au	UNIX Audio
.mid or .midi	Musical Instrument Digital Inteface
.mp3	MPEG Audio Layer 3
.wav	Wave Form
.wma	Windows Media Audio

Video File Formats

File Format	Description
.asf	Advanced Streaming Format
.avi	Audio Video Interface
.mpg or .mpeg	Moving Picture Experts Group
.swf	Flash Video
.wmv	Windows Media Video

QuickTime Videos

Unfortunately, you are not able to insert Apple QuickTime video files (those files with a .mov extension) into your presentation.

If you need to play a QuickTime video during your presentation, the easiest way of achieving this is to create a hyperlink to the actual .mov file, then click on that link during the presentation.

The other option would be to convert the .mov file to one of the supported video file formats. However, this process requires additional software that is not provided as part of the Microsoft Office suite, and can sometimes be quite complicated.

Hot tip

If you want to view your photos in full screen, select Fit to slide from the Picture layout box.

Hot tip

If you want to add captions to a photo, you must first specify a layout for the pictures in the album.

Hot tip

To make the presentation look more like a photo album, choose a frame shape after you have chosen the picture layout.

8 Reviewing & Proofing

This chapter will guide you through the process of checking and reviewing your presentation.

Office Language Settings

When you type a word, PowerPoint will identify that word as belonging to a specific language, based on whatever you have set as your keyboard layout.

This language is then used to determine which dictionary to use, how AutoCorrect works, and whatever rules are used to check grammar.

There may be times when you want to use a word, or words, that belong to a different language. You can tell PowerPoint what language those are in.

Hot tip

You can also change the language settings, including the primary editing language, by clicking on Microsoft Office 2010 Language Settings in the Microsoft Office Tools program menu.

1 Highlight the word you want to set the language to

2 Click the Review tab and click Language, then select the Set Proofing Language button

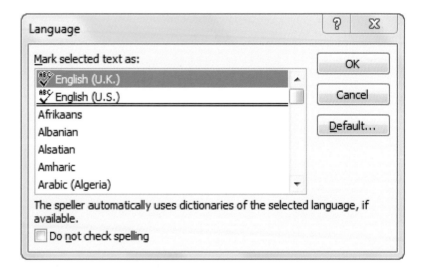

3 Select the language you want to use

4 Click OK

You can also choose not to check the spelling of that word, or piece of text, by placing a tick in the Do not check spelling box.

Don't forget

Changing the default language will affect the presentation you are working on, and all future presentations.

Office Proofing Options

To save time, and also the need to keep repeating proofing tasks, you can set the defaults on how PowerPoint 2010 will correct and format your presentations.

These include AutoCorrect and spelling, specifically in PowerPoint, both of which will be covered later in this chapter. There are also settings which affect any installed Office programs.

1 Click the File tab, then click on Options

2 Click Proofing

3 Change any settings you feel the need to change

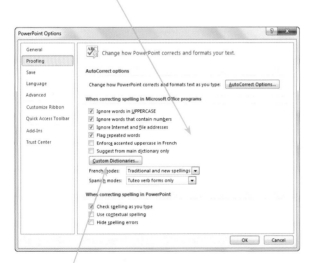

4 Click Custom Dictionaries to add, remove, or create a new dictionary. You can also edit the word list from here

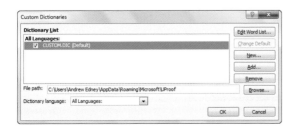

Don't forget

Some of the changes you make in the Proofing options will affect any Office 2010 applications that are installed on your system, not just PowerPoint 2010.

Hot tip

If you have added a lot of words to a dictionary, you can give a copy of it to others for them to use, in order to save time and ensure the words are spelt correctly.

Hot tip

You can buy or download custom dictionaries and add them to PowerPoint, saving you from adding lots of new words.

AutoCorrect

AutoCorrect is one of those functions that is just amazing. What it does is automatically detect and correct any misspelt words, or incorrect capitalization. It also aids the quick insertion of symbols, such as the copyright symbol, by just typing (c).

Hot tip

AutoCorrect is a very useful tool indeed. It will save you hours of having to go and correct little mistakes.

1 Click the File tab, then click on Options

2 Click Proofing, then click AutoCorrect Options

3 Check or uncheck the relevant options, to suit your needs

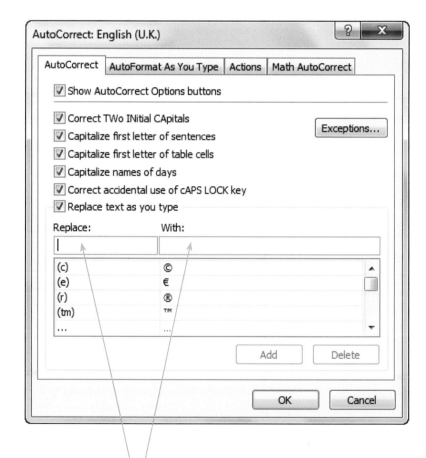

Hot tip

There may be words that you do not want to have capitalized using AutoCorrect. If this is the case, use the Exceptions button to add them.

120

4 You can even add your own words and changes

AutoFormat As You Type

This feature replaces certain types of text entries with something that looks flashier.

If you were to type :-), it would be replaced with

There are also options that are applied as you type, for example, automatic bulleted and numbered lists, instead of you having to type the next number in a list, PowerPoint adds it for you.

1 Click the AutoFormat As You Type tab

Don't forget

If you don't want your Internet URLs and your network paths shown with hyperlinks automatically, uncheck the Internet and network paths with hyperlinks box.

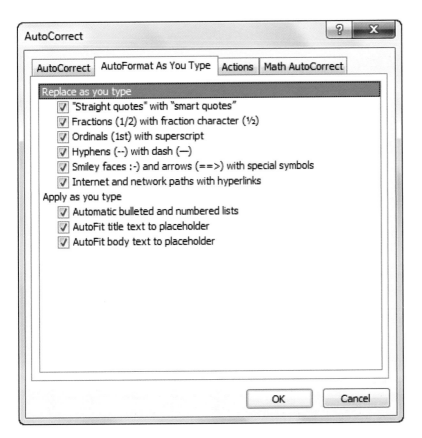

2 Check or uncheck the relevant options, to suit your needs

Spelling

Checking your spelling throughout your presentation is very important. The last thing you want is to have spent several hours preparing a very important presentation, only to find you have made some spelling mistakes.

Automatic Checking

Some people like to see if they have made a mistake as they are typing. If you are one of these people, then you will want to use the automatic checking capability.

When you type a word that is spelt incorrectly, or is not in the dictionary, it is underlined with a red wavy line.

As you can see from the pictur

Don't forget

Not all words will be in the dictionary. For example, product names, or words specific to you or your organization, may not appear.

1 Click the right mouse button over the word, PowerPoint will make suggestions as to what the word might be

2 Click on the word in the list if it appears. If it is the correct spelling, click Add to Dictionary to use it again

picture

Ignore All

Add to Dictionary

Spelling...

Cut

Copy

Paste Options:

A

Hot tip

Any words that you know are correctly spelt, or words that are not in the dictionary, should be added to the dictionary. This will save you time in the future if you ever use those words again.

Enabling or Disabling Automatic checking

To enable or disable automatic checking:

1 Click the File tab

2 Click on Options

3 Select Proofing

4 Check or uncheck the Check spelling as you type box

Manual Checking

If you are not one of those people who likes to see when they have made a mistake as they make it, or if you find those wavy lines annoying or distracting, you can perform a manual spell check at any time.

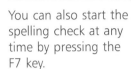
Hot tip

You can also start the spelling check at any time by pressing the F7 key.

1 Click the Review tab

Spelling Research Thesaurus

Proofing

2 Click the Spelling icon, from the Proofing commands menu

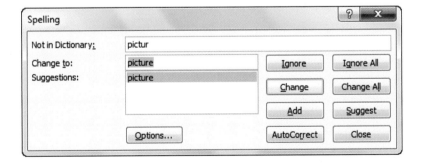

Hot tip

If your have spelt a word incorrectly a number of times, use the Change All button instead of checking each one in turn. The same goes for using the Ignore All button if you don't want to change them.

3 If a word is highlighted and one of the suggestions is correct, highlight that suggestion and click Change

4 You can add the word to your dictionary by clicking Add

5 When you have completed the spelling check, click Close

Researching

Research

Should you need to research a word or topic, PowerPoint 2010 has the ability to search through various reference materials, such as online services, dictionaries and encyclopedia.

1 Click the Review tab and select the Research button, from the Proofing commands menu

2 Enter the word or phrase in the Search for: box

3 Select the references, or leave on the default All Reference Books

4 Click the Start searching button

You will now be presented with the results, which you can scroll through, depending on the number of hits.

Thesaurus

There is also a thesaurus function which, when used, will suggest other words with a similar meaning to the one you select or type.

1 Highlight a word, then click the Review tab and select the Thesaurus button from the Proofing commands menu

2 Enter the word or phrase in the entry box

3 Select the references, or leave on the default All Reference Books, and click the Start searching button, in the same way as you did for researching

Options

There are a number of options you can change, relating to both the research functions and the thesaurus, such as the addition or removal of services, and also updating existing services.

1 Click Research options at the bottom of the Research window

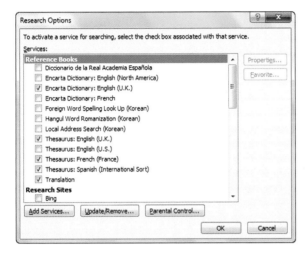

2 Check or uncheck the boxes next to the available services, as required, or select the Add Services button to add, or the Update/Remove button to perform those functions

3 You can learn more about any Service by selecting it and then clicking on the Properties button

Translation

PowerPoint gives you the ability to translate words, or short phrases, from one language to another, using the Research function.

Don't forget

Once you have your translated word or phase, you must type it into your presentation yourself, as it is not entered automatically.

1 Click the Review tab and click the Translate button from the Language commands menu, then select Translate Selected Text

2 Type the word or phase in the Search for: box

3 Choose the language to translate from and to

4 Click the green Start Searching button to begin

5 Review the translation

Hot tip

Additional language packs can be purchased and downloaded from the Microsoft Office Online website http://office.microsoft.com.

Translation Options

These options allow you to choose whether or not to use the online dictionary, including when to use it, and also shows you the available language pairs you can use.

The Bilingual Dictionary is the locally installed dictionary.

1 Click on Translation options

2 Check or uncheck the options, as necessary

Comments

By using the Comments feature of PowerPoint 2010, you can easily add comments to a slide. These comments can be used for review purposes, or as notes to yourself. Each comment has a unique number and initials of the person who left the comment.

Adding a Review Comment

1 Click the Review tab and select New Comment, from the Comments commands menu

2 Type your comment and click anywhere outside of the comment box

3 Move the comment box to a specific location on the screen, if required

Editing a Review Comment

1 Click on the review comment you want to edit

2 Click the Edit Comment button

Deleting a Review Comment

1 Click on the review comment you want to delete

2 Click the Delete button

Hot tip

Use the Next and Previous buttons on the Comments command menu, to easily step between comments, rather than clicking on each individual comment.

Hot tip

To read comments that have been added to the presentation, click the Show Markup button on the comments menu.

Beware

If you are used to using previous versions of PowerPoint, you will notice that the Send for Review option no longer exists. To perform this function now, you must email the presentation. Reviewers can use the comments feature and then email it back to you.

Outline View

Outline View gives you the ability to just view the text entries on each slide, without any backgrounds, graphics, or other additions. This can make it very easy to quickly scroll through and check for errors, including spelling mistakes and formatting problems.

1 Select Outline on the PowerPoint window

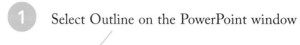

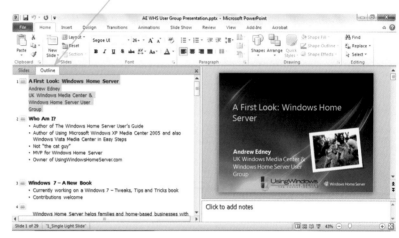

Print Outline View

You can also print the outline view, if you find it easier to check the presentation on paper rather than on the screen.

1 Click on the File tab

2 Click on Print

3 Select Outline View, from the Print what drop-down list

9 Creating Slide Shows

This chapter will tell you everything you need to know about creating slide shows of your presentations, including adding narration and creating self-running presentation, for use in kiosks and demonstrations.

Slide Shows

Once you have finished putting your presentation together, it's time to actually present it, or, at the very least, run through it to make sure you are happy with it, and see what it will look like from the audiences' perspective.

Starting a Slide Show

1 Click on the Slide Show tab

2 From the Start Slide Show group, select either From Beginning, to start from the first slide, or From Current Slide, to start from the current point in the presentation

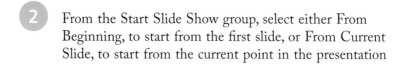

3 Run through your presentation, or press ESC to end the slide show

Set Up Options

There are a number of options you can change for your slide shows. These include the show type, how you will advance through the slide, what color your default pen will be, and even the slide show resolution, among others.

1 Click on the Slide Show tab

2 From the Set Up Slide Show group, select Set Up Slide Show, or press the arrow at the bottom-right of the group

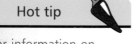

Hot tip

It is a very good idea to run through your presentation, to ensure that the presentation flows as you want it to, and that you have covered everything you needed to.

Hot tip

For information on Broadcasting your Slide Show over the Internet, look at Chapter 11.

Show Type

These options allow you to choose how the presentation will be displayed for your audience.

Show Slides

These options allow you to choose which slides are shown, including the option to specify custom shows.

Don't forget

The list of available pen colors is only available to you if the show type selected is Presented by a speaker (full screen).

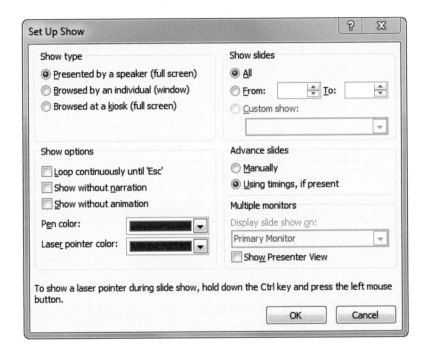

Hot tip

In order to speed up the rendering of graphics in your presentation, check the Use hardware graphics acceleration box, if the graphics card in your computer supports it.

131

Show Options

These options allow you to specify how sounds and animations are run, and you can select the default pen color.

Advance Slides

These options determine how the slides move from one to the next.

Multiple Monitors

These options are used to specify which monitor to display the slide show on, if you have multiple monitors available for your presentation.

Beware

Increasing the resolution makes the quality of the presentation better, but there may be a performance hit in doing so.

Rehearsing and Timings

A lot of times, when you are presenting, you will have a limited amount of time available to actually deliver the presentation.

You can have PowerPoint 2010 time you while you are rehearsing your presentation, so that you know how long you have taken. You can then have PowerPoint 2010 record this time, so that you can advance your slides automatically, or even use the times to create a self-running presentation.

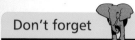

Don't forget

As soon as you click the Rehearse Timings button, the timer begins – so make sure you are ready to present.

1 Click on the Slide Show tab and select Rehearse Timings from the Set Up group

The Rehearsal toolbar enables you to pause the presentation or advance to the next slide.

You can also see the time on current slide, and also the total time.

Hot tip

If you want your slides to advance automatically when you present, ensure the Use Rehearsed Timings box is checked. Likewise, if you don't want them to advance, ensure it is unchecked.

2 Work through the rehearsal of your presentation

3 Press ESC to finish the rehearsal, and decide if you want to use the newly recorded slide timings when you view your slide show

Writing on Slides

During your slide show, you may want to write on the slides, as though you were using a whiteboard. You can use different types of pens and colors, and write anything you want, including underlining, circling, or any other freehand writing.

1 At any point during your slide show, when you are on a slide you wish to write on, either press the right mouse button and highlight Pointer Options, or, at the bottom-left of the screen, click on the pen icon

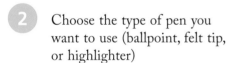

2 Choose the type of pen you want to use (ballpoint, felt tip, or highlighter)

3 Choose the ink color, if you want to change it

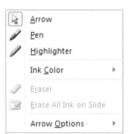

4 Hold down the left mouse button and drag the chosen pen over the slide to write with it

133

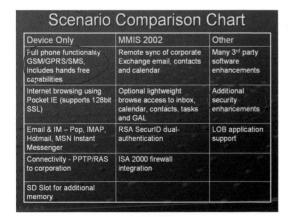

Scenario Comparison Chart

Device Only	MMIS 2002	Other
Full phone functionality GSM/GPRS/SMS, Includes hands free capabilities	Remote sync of corporate Exchange email, contacts and calendar	Many 3rd party software enhancements
Internet browsing using Pocket IE (supports 128bit SSL)	Optional lightweight browse access to inbox, calendar, contacts, tasks and GAL	Additional security enhancements
Email & IM – Pop, IMAP, Hotmail, MSN Instant Messenger	RSA SecurID dual-authentication	LOB application support
Connectivity - PPTP/RAS to corporation	ISA 2000 firewall integration	
SD Slot for additional memory		

Using Multiple Monitors

You can now deliver a presentation on more than one monitor. For example, you can have your audience view the presentation on one screen, while you view it on another. This other view is known as the Presenter View.

Presenter View

When you use Presenter View, you can run other programs, or different views of your presentation, without your audience being able to see what you are viewing. You can also:

- See Preview text, which shows you what will appear on the screen with your next click

- Use thumbnails of your slides to create a customized presentation, as you are presenting

- View your Speaker notes, which are displayed in large clear type to make it easy for you to read

Extending Your Desktop

Before you can use the Presenter View, you have to extend your desktop onto the second monitor.

Don't forget

You will need a computer that has multiple monitor capability to use these features.

Don't forget

PowerPoint 2010 supports the use of a maximum of two monitors, even if your computer can support more.

1   Press the right mouse button on your Windows 7 desktop and select Screen resolution

2   Select Display Settings from the list

3   Select 2 for the second monitor

4   Choose Extend these displays, from the Multiple Displays drop down list

5   Set the resolution and colors, as appropriate, for your second monitor and click OK

Enabling Presenter View

Now that you have enabled multiple monitors in Windows 7, you can change the presentation resolution, decide which monitor to show the presentation on, and whether or not to enable Presenter View.

1 Click on the Slide Show tab to display the Monitors group

2 Set the resolution, or leave as Use Current Resolution

3 Select the monitor to Show Presentation On

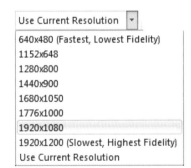

4 Check the Show Presenter View box

5 Start the slide show

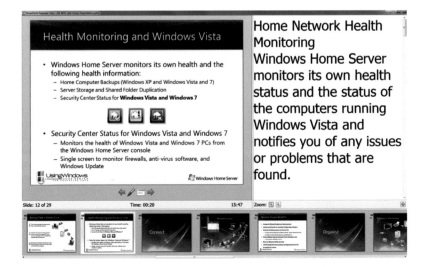

Narration

Narration is a great way to enhance your presentation. It can be used to aid you while you are presenting, or it is best used for self-running presentations, CD packaged presentations, or even for people who could not attend the actual presentation but want to hear what you had to say.

You can record your narration at any time, before your presentation, after your presentation, or even during it, should you wish to record any comments or questions from your audience.

Recording a Narration

1 Select the slide you want to begin the narration from

2 From the Slide Show tab, click Record Slide show and then choose where to start the narration from

3 Select what you want to record, before you begin recording

4 Click the Start Recording button

5 Speak clearly into the microphone

6 Use the Enter key to move to the next slide

7 Press the Escape key to finish recording

Laser Pointer

A new feature of PowerPoint 2010 is the Laser Pointer. During a slide show, you can use the mouse to make a laser pointer appear on the screen, instead of actually having to have a seperate laser pointer aimed at the display you are using.

1 From the Slide Show tab, click on Slide Show Options

2 Select the color of the laser pointer (you can choose from red, green or blue)

4 Click OK

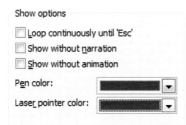

Hot tip

Make sure that you choose a color for the laser pointer that will show up on your presentation — for example, if you have a blue slide backgroud, choosing blue for the laser pointer may make it difficult to see it.

137

4 Start the slide show and hold down the CTRL key and the left mouse button to display the laser pointer

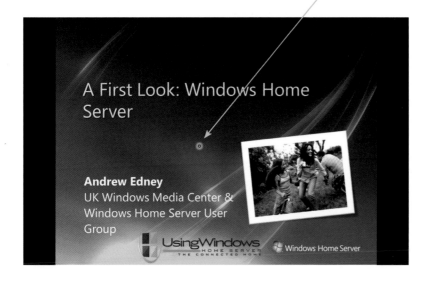

Slide Transitions

When you change from one slide to the next, this is called a slide transition. You can choose from a large number of different transitions, add sounds, decide how fast the transition is, and much more.

Using the Same Transition for All Slides

1 Click on the Transitions tab

Hot tip

Try a number of different transitions and speeds – some may be better for your presentation than others. You can easily change them, then click Preview to have a look.

138

2 Click on a slide transition icon from the Transition To This Slide group, or click on the More button to see all available transitions

Hot tip

Each transition may have a different transition effect, so it is worth having a look at each one, to see which is the best one for the presentation you are working on.

3 Select a transistion effect, or leave it on the default

4 Set the transition duration, or leave it on the default

5   Click on the Apply to All button to set that transition and speed throughout your presentation

Using Different Transitions for Each Slide

1   Select the slide you want to transition to

2   Click on the Transitions tab

3   Click on a slide transition icon from the Transition To This Slide group, or click on the More button to see all available transitions

4   Set the Transition duration, or leave it on the default

5   Repeat steps 1 – 4 for each slide you want to use a different transition for

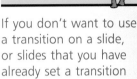

Don't forget

If you don't want to use a transition on a slide, or slides that you have already set a transition for, choose No Transition from the available transitions menu.

139

Adding Sounds to Transitions

You can add sounds to the transitions as well.

1   Select the slide you want to add the sound to

2   Click on the Transition Sound option list and choose a sound, or select Other Sound to add your own

Advancing Slides

You can choose to have the slide advance on a click of the mouse (which is the default action) or you can set an amount of time before the slide automatically transitions.

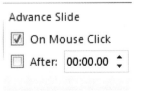

Custom Slide Shows

You can use a custom slide show to adapt an existing presentation for other audiences, without the need to take a complete copy of the presentation and change it, thus having multiple copies.

There are two different types of custom slide shows: basic shows and hyperlinked shows.

Basic Shows

Basic custom shows are separate presentations, or presentations that only contain a subset of slides from your chosen presentation. For example, the presentation to your boss might contain all the slides you have created, but the presentation to your staff may only contain some of them.

1 Click on the Slide Show tab

2 Click the arrow on the Custom Slide Show button

3 Click on the Custom Shows button

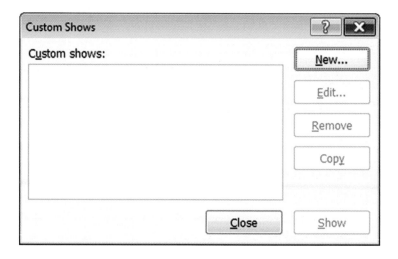

4 Click on the New button, or select a custom show from the list and click Edit

140

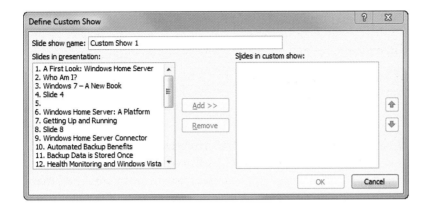

5 Highlight the slides from the presentation and click the Add button to add them to the custom show

6 Use the up and down arrows to change the sequence of the slides in the custom show

7 Give your custom slide show a name and click OK

8 You can then preview your new custom slide show by clicking the Show button

Hot tip

To select multiple slides at the same time, hold down the SHIFT button if the slides are in sequence, or the CTRL button if they are not.

Playing Custom Shows

You can play a custom slide show by selecting it from the list of available custom shows.

To play a custom slide show:

1 Click on the Slide Show tab

2 Click the arrow on the Custom Slide Show button

3 Click on the name of the custom slide show to play it

Hyperlinked Slide Shows

Hyperlinked custom slide shows allow you to navigate to one or more sections within the presentation, via a link.

1 Ensure you have created all your custom shows as described in the Basic Shows section

2 Select the text, or an object that you want to use as the link

3 Click on the Insert tab, then choose Hyperlink from the Links group

Hyperlink Action

Links

4 On the Link to list, click on Place in This Document

5 Scroll down the Select a place in this document list to Custom Shows

6 Click on the show you want to link to and place a check in the Show and return box, then click OK

The text you selected to link to will now be underlined. To launch the hyperlink show, just click on the word during the main presentation.

Self-Running Presentations

You may want your presentation to be running without the need for you to be there, for example, in a reception area, at a trade show, or in a kiosk.

You can even set the presentation so that other people cannot make changes to it. Effectively, you are removing most of the PowerPoint controls from being used.

Self-running presentations will also restart when they have completed their run through and, if you have a slide that requires manual input to continue, it will continue automatically after a period of five minutes.

Options

There are a number of options to consider with self-running presentations. These include:

- The use of hyperlinks and action buttons to guide viewers through the presentation

- Using narration to talk viewers through the presentation, as if you were there presenting it to them yourself, as described earlier in this chapter

- The use of timings, so that viewers have enough time to view each slide, without feeling rushed or getting bored, also described earlier in this chapter

Kiosk Mode

There is a special option available for slide shows, referred to as Browsed at a kiosk. This enables your presentation to be displayed in full screen, and enables the viewer to have additional control over the viewing, if you give them that ability.

1. Click on the Slide Show tab

2. Click the Set Up Slide Show button to launch the Set Up Show dialog box

3. Change the show type to Browsed at a kiosk (full screen), then click OK

Don't forget

Keep in mind where the self-running presentation will be played. This will help you to determine the best elements to add to your presentation.

Hot tip

You can also package your self-running presentation to run from a CD. See Package for CD in chapter 11.

Don't forget

Make sure to set automatic timings, hyperlinks or action buttons when using kiosk mode, or the presentation will get stuck on the first slide.

Keyboard Shortcuts

When you are presenting your slide show, there are a number of keyboard shortcuts that you can use.

Below are a list of some of the more commonly used ones.

Function	Press
Start a presentation from the beginning	Mouse buttons
Next animation or go to next slide	N, ENTER
Previous animation or go to previous slide	P, BACKSPACE
Go to slide number...	number+ENTER
Display a black slide or return from one	B
Display a white slide or return from one	W
Stop or restart an automatic presentation	S
End the presentation	ESC
Return to the first slide	1+ENTER
Display the shortcut menu	shift+F10
Perform mouse click on selected hyperlink	ENTER
Go to the first or next hyperlink	TAB
Go to the previous or last hyperlink	SHIFT+TAB
Erase drawing	E
View task bar	CTRL+T

For some functions, there are a number of possible keys that could be used. For example, going to the next slide (as shown above, using the N or the ENTER key) can also be achieved by using page down, right arrow, down arrow, or even the spacebar.

The Slide Sorter

If you want to view your presentation and change the order of the slides easily, you can use the Slide Sorter view.

When you select the Slide Sorter, all of the slides in your presentation are displayed in sequence, as thumbnails.

You can then easily drag slides into a new position within the presentation, or even delete any of them.

1 Click on the Slide Sorter icon near the bottom-right of the screen

2 Scroll through the slides in the presentation, until you come to one you want to move or delete

3 Click on the slide to highlight it

4 If you want to move it to a different position, hold the left mouse button down and drag the slide to wherever you want it, then release the button

5 If you want to delete the slide, or add a new slide, press the right mouse button and then click either New Slide or Delete Slide

6 Click on the Normal icon near the bottom of the screen to return to the normal view

Slide Show Options

There are a number of different options that can be set for how PowerPoint performs when using Slide Shows. These options are:

- Show menu on right mouse click – enables or disables the shortcut menu being displayed during a slide show, enabling you to select menu options without having to stop the slide show itself

- Show pop-up toolbar – enables or disables the toolbar that appears at the bottom of the screen, when displaying a slide show in full screen

- Prompt to keep ink annotations when exiting – enables or disables the prompt to save any annotations that have been made to slides during the slide show

- End with black slide – will display a black slide at the end of the presentation. If this option is not selected, when the presentation ends you will be returned to PowerPoint

1. Click on the File tab and select Options

2. Click on Advanced

3. Scroll down to the section called Slide Show

Slide Show

- ☑ Show menu on right mouse click ⓘ
- ☑ Show popup toolbar ⓘ
- ☑ Prompt to keep ink annotations when exiting
- ☑ End with black slide

4. Check or clear the Slide Show options boxes, depending on what options you want to enable or disable

5. Click OK to save the changes

10 Saving Your Presentation

This chapter will tell you everything you need to know, in order to save in some of the various formats available, including earlier versions of PowerPoint.

Saving a Presentation

Saving a presentation could not be easier. Now that you have finished your presentation, or have got to a stage where you want to save your progress, you have a number of different options available to you.

1 Click the File tab and select Save, or click the floppy disk icon to initiate the save process

2 In the Save In box, select the location where you want your presentation saved

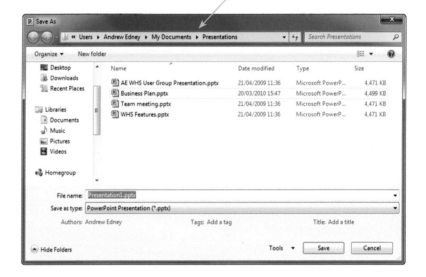

3 If you need to, create a new folder to save your presentation to

4 In the File name box, enter a name for your presentation

5 Click Save

This will save the presentation in the default .pptx format, first introduced with PowerPoint 2007.

Choosing a Different Type

By default, when you save a presentation, it is saved as a PowerPoint 2010 .pptx type.

You can also save as many different types of files.

1 Perform the same steps as you did to save a presentation, only this time do not click Save just yet

2 Click the drop-down arrow on the Save as type box, to reveal all the possible file types you can save as

PowerPoint Presentation (*.pptx)
PowerPoint Macro-Enabled Presentation (*.pptm)
PowerPoint 97-2003 Presentation (*.ppt)
PDF (*.pdf)
XPS Document (*.xps)
PowerPoint Template (*.potx)
PowerPoint Macro-Enabled Template (*.potm)
PowerPoint 97-2003 Template (*.pot)
Office Theme (*.thmx)
PowerPoint Show (*.ppsx)
PowerPoint Macro-Enabled Show (*.ppsm)
PowerPoint 97-2003 Show (*.pps)
PowerPoint Add-In (*.ppam)
PowerPoint 97-2003 Add-In (*.ppa)
PowerPoint XML Presentation (*.xml)
Windows Media Video (*.wmv)
GIF Graphics Interchange Format (*.gif)
JPEG File Interchange Format (*.jpg)
PNG Portable Network Graphics Format (*.png)
TIFF Tag Image File Format (*.tif)
Device Independent Bitmap (*.bmp)
Windows Metafile (*.wmf)
Enhanced Windows Metafile (*.emf)
Outline/RTF (*.rtf)
PowerPoint Picture Presentation (*.pptx)
OpenDocument Presentation (*.odp)

Hot tip

Make sure you select the correct type for the presentation you want to save.

3 Select the required file type from the drop-down list

4 Click Save and follow any on-screen instructions

Saving as a PDF

PDF is Adobe's Portable Document Format. It is used to share documents, and it keeps the format exactly the same as that of the original, for ease of viewing and printing. The ability to save a presentation as a PDF with PowerPoint 2010 is very useful for when you want to send a presentation to someone to either review, or as an electronic handout following a presentation.

Saving as a PDF

1 Follow the same steps as used before to save a presentation, only this time select PDF from the Save as type menu, or click the File tab and click Save As, then choose PDF or XPS

Don't forget

In order to view a PDF once you have created it, you must have Adobe Reader installed on your computer. You can download it from http://www.adobe.com, if you don't already have it installed.

2 You can have the PDF open automatically once it has been created, by selecting the Open file after publishing box

3 Set any optimization you want – Standard (which is the default) is probably sufficient for your purposes, as this is the setting for publishing online and printing

4 At this point, you can click Save to complete the process, or you can select the Options tab to change or set any additional options you may wish to use

Options

For most people, the default option settings will be sufficient. However, if you want to change what is being published, you can do so quite easily.

These settings include:

- Which slides to publish (all, the current slide, or a selection)

- The ability to choose the format and layout (slides, handouts, notes pages, or outline views) of what is published

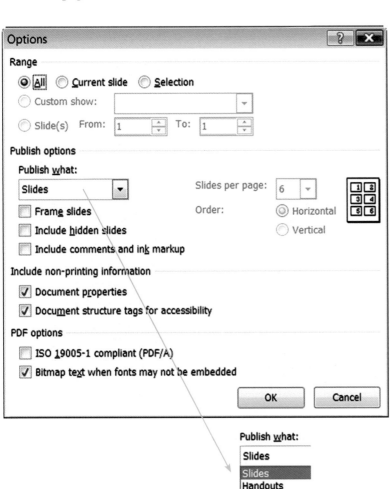

Beware

Any animations, transitions, or sound and video, will not be preserved when you create the PDF.

Compatibility Checker

PowerPoint 2010 uses new file formats, and contains lots of new features, and not everyone you will want to share your files with will have 2010, there is a risk that part, or all of your presentation, may not be compatible with earlier versions of PowerPoint.

This is where the Compatibility Checker comes in to play.

When you select Compatibility Checker, or save a presentation in a down-level format (PowerPoint 97–2003), and your presentation contains some of the new features, you will be presented with the Compatibility Checker.

The results of the compatibility checker will display:

- Any incompatibilities in the presentation

- What the behavior will be when viewed in earlier versions

- How many occurrences of each specific type exist

Hot tip

When working on presentations in compatibility mode, where the presentation is in a PowerPoint 97–2003 format, the Compatibility Checker will run automatically when you save your presentation.

1. Click on the File tab and then click Check for Issues, from the Info area

2. Select Check Compatibility

Check Compatibility
Check for features not supported by earlier versions of PowerPoint.

Don't forget

Always read what is displayed in the Compatibility Checker summary, as you don't want people not to be able to view your presentations!

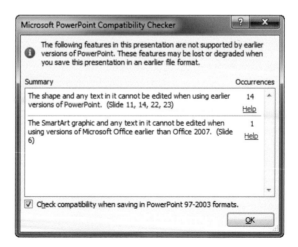

New Formats

You may have noticed, if you have already saved a presentation, or tried to open a presentation, that PowerPoint 2010 uses a different file format, called PowerPoint XML (.pptx). If you are familiar with PowerPoint 2007, then you may have seen this file format already.

This new format saves presentations as much smaller files than .ppt's used to, and there is also improved recovery of corrupt or damaged files.

There are a number of XML file types supported by PowerPoint 2010, along with a number of existing file types.

New file types and extensions

The following table highlights the new XML file types, and their extensions:

Extension	XML File Type
.pptx	PowerPoint Presentation
.pptm	Macro-enabled presentation
.potx	Template
.potm	Macro-enabled template
.ppam	Macro-enabled add-in
.ppsx	Show
.ppsm	Macro-enabled show
.sldx	Slide
.sldm	Macro-enabled slide
.thmx	Office theme
.pdf	PDF file
.xps	XPS document
.pps	Show

Don't forget

Users of earlier versions of PowerPoint, before PowerPoint 2007, will not be able to open these new file types.

Default Saving Options

You can tell PowerPoint the format of the files that you save as a default, including setting the time for autosaves and default file locations.

The format choices are either PowerPoint Presentation, which is the new PowerPoint 2010 format, PowerPoint Macro-Enable Presentation or PowerPoint Presentation 97–2003 or OpenDocument Presentation.

Don't forget

Only change these settings if you think you need to. The default settings are usually good enough for most people.

Hot tip

If you are going to be sharing a considerable amount of presentations with users of earlier versions of PowerPoint, you might want to consider setting the format default to PowerPoint Presentation 97–2003.

1 Click the File tab and select Options

2 Click Save, from the left-hand column

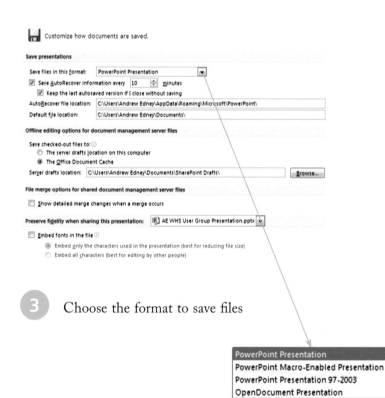

Customize how documents are saved.

Save presentations

Save files in this format: PowerPoint Presentation

☑ Save AutoRecover information every 10 minutes

☑ Keep the last autosaved version if I close without saving

AutoRecover file location: C:\Users\Andrew Edney\AppData\Roaming\Microsoft\PowerPoint\

Default file location: C:\Users\Andrew Edney\Documents\

Offline editing options for document management server files

Save checked-out files to:

○ The server drafts location on this computer

◉ The Office Document Cache

Server drafts location: C:\Users\Andrew Edney\Documents\SharePoint Drafts\   Browse...

File merge options for shared document management server files

☐ Show detailed merge changes when a merge occurs

Preserve fidelity when sharing this presentation: AE WHS User Group Presentation.pptx

☐ Embed fonts in the file

◉ Embed only the characters used in the presentation (best for reducing file size)

○ Embed all characters (best for editing by other people)

3 Choose the format to save files

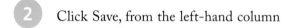

PowerPoint Presentation
PowerPoint Macro-Enabled Presentation
PowerPoint Presentation 97-2003
OpenDocument Presentation

4 Set the time for saving autorecover information

5 Change the default file location if necessary

Save to Web

You can choose to save your PowerPoint presentation to your Windows Live webspace. From there, you can give permission to other people to view it, download it, and so on.

To save your presentation to the web:

1 Click the File tab and select Save & Send

2 Click Save to Web

3 You may be asked to Sign In to Windows Live - just click Sign In and enter your Windows Live ID credentials

4 Choose where to save your presentation, or click Save As

Don't forget

You need to be connected to the Internet in order to use the Save to Web feature.

Don't forget

If you don't have a Windows Live account, you can easily sign up for one.

Hot tip

You might want to create a new set of folders that you can assign different permissions to, that way you don't have to give permissions to an existing folder.

Saving in an Earlier Format

If you want to save your presentation in an earlier PowerPoint format, in order to share with someone who does not have PowerPoint 2010 or PowerPoint 2007, it is very easy to do.

If you have used any of the new features of PowerPoint 2010 in your presentation, they may not be available in the 97–2003 presentation.

1. Click the File tab and then click Save As

2. Select PowerPoint 97–2003 Presentation

Beware

PowerPoint 97–2003 does not recognize the new SmartArt graphics and visual objects of 2010. These will automatically be converted to bitmaps, to maintain their appearance.

3. In the Save In box, select the location where you want your presentation saved

4. In the File name box, enter a name for your presentation

5. Click Save

Compatibility with Earlier Versions of PowerPoint

Users of PowerPoint 2000, XP or 2003 can download a file format converter patch from Microsoft Office Online, which will give them the ability to open, edit and save files using the new XML format. The minimum installed service pack to use the converter is as follows:

Don't forget

You must download and install the patch before you can use the new formats.

- Office 2000 Service Pack 3

- Office XP Service Pack 3

- Office 2003 Service Pack 1

11 Sharing Presentations

This chapter will guide you through the process of preparing your presentation for sharing with others. This includes checking for personal information in the presentation, printing and publishing, and even writing it to CD or creating a video.

Presentation Properties

Each document has a number of properties associated with it. These properties are often referred to as metadata, and include:

- Presentation title
- Author information
- Keywords

Properties

1 Press the File tab and choose Info, then click Properties and select Show Document Panel

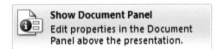

Show Document Panel
Edit properties in the Document
Panel above the presentation.

2 This brings up the standard properties box. As you can see, some of the fields are populated by default, such as author name

Standard properties enable you to enter metadata for:

- Author
- Subject
- Category
- Comments
- Title
- Keywords
- Status

3 Enter any information you want in these boxes. The keywords field is particularly useful

Hot tip

By entering values in the various properties boxes, you can organize presentations and make it easier to find what you are searching for later, by using that metadata.

Advanced Properties

Choosing the advanced properties option gives you a greater level of control over what you can add or change.

1 Click on Properties to bring up the Advanced Properties box

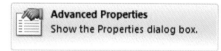

Advanced properties gives you additional information, including:

● What template is being used

● Various statistics on the presentation

● Document contents and custom fields

2 Navigate the tabs and enter any information you want

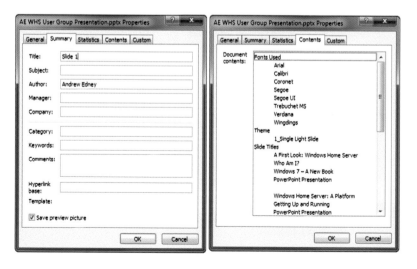

3 Click OK to finish

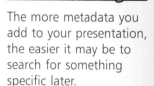

Inspecting Documents

As you are planning on sharing your presentation, it would be a good idea to check that there is no personal information, or hidden data, within it. This hidden data could contain information about you or your organization that you don't want to share.

Document Inspector

1 Press the File tab, click on Info, then click Check for Issues and select Inspect Document, to launch the Document Inspector

> **Inspect Document**
> Check the presentation for hidden properties or personal information.

2 Choose the types of content that you want to inspect for by placing a check in the box for each one

160

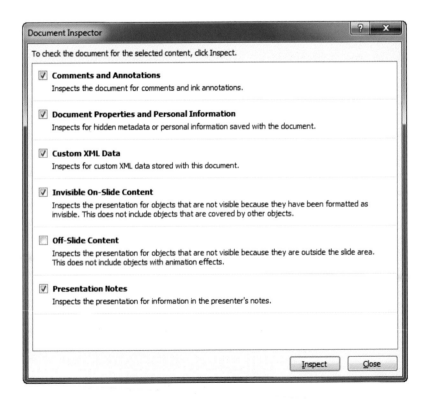

Document Inspector

To check the document for the selected content, click Inspect.

☑ **Comments and Annotations**
Inspects the document for comments and ink annotations.

☑ **Document Properties and Personal Information**
Inspects for hidden metadata or personal information saved with the document.

☑ **Custom XML Data**
Inspects for custom XML data stored with this document.

☑ **Invisible On-Slide Content**
Inspects the presentation for objects that are not visible because they have been formatted as invisible. This does not include objects that are covered by other objects.

☐ **Off-Slide Content**
Inspects the presentation for objects that are not visible because they are outside the slide area. This does not include objects with animation effects.

☑ **Presentation Notes**
Inspects the presentation for information in the presenter's notes.

Inspect   Close

3 Click Inspect to begin the inspection process

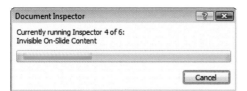

4 Check the results carefully, and click the Remove All button against whichever type of hidden content you want to remove

161

5 You can then choose to recheck the document by clicking the Reinspect button

6 Click Close to finish the inspection process

Marking as Final

The Mark As Final option in PowerPoint 2010 is used to make the presentation read-only, preventing changes from being made once you have shared it.

Mark As Final

1 Press the File tab, then click Protect Presentation and select Mark As Final

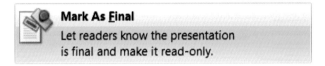

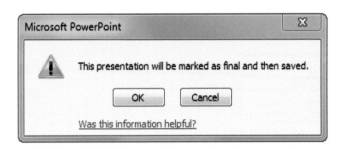

162

2 Click OK to mark the presentation as final and save it. The process for saving a presentation should be followed as normal

Unmarking As Final

If you need to edit the presentation, or add to it, you will need to run through the same process again, only this time unmark it as final.

1 Press the File tab, then click Protect Presentation and select Mark As Final

2 Continue working on the presentation

3 When you are ready to Mark As Final again, run through the steps listed above

Package for CD

One of the easiest ways to share your presentation with others is on CD. When you use the Package for CD functionality in PowerPoint 2010, you also have a number of options, including the ability to make the presentation or presentations self-running packages, without the need for users to have PowerPoint.

Don't forget

Make sure you have a blank CD in the drive, ready to be written.

Package for CD

1 Press the File tab, choose Save & Send and select Package Presentation for CD

2 Click on Package for CD

3 Enter a name for the CD and click Add Files to add additional presentations to be written

Hot tip

The files to be copied to the CD are shown. If you have more than one file to be copied, you can change the Play Order. This is particularly useful if you set the CD option to play the presentation automatically, in the specified order.

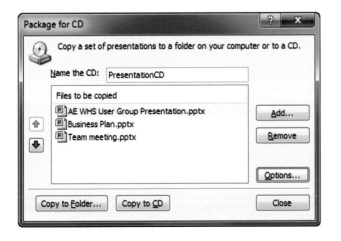

Hot tip

If you want to make your CD presentations look slicker, you can set them to play automatically when a user inserts the CD, and have them play in the specified order, if that is important to the content.

Don't forget

It's always a good idea to inspect the presentations for personal information, or hidden data, before sharing them.

Beware

Linked files can be used by hackers to introduce elements to your presentations that you do not want to have.

4 Click Options to set the various additional options available

5 Here you can change the package type, whether to include linked files, set passwords, even inspect the presentation prior to writing it to CD

6 After you have made your required changes, click OK

7 Click Copy to CD to begin writing the CD

8 Make sure a Blank CD is in your writer, otherwise you will see a warning

9 After the CD has finished writing, you have the option to write another CD with the same files

Viewing from CD

When you have a CD that contains a packaged set of PowerPoint files, all you need to do to view them is put the CD in the drive.

1 Put the CD in the CD drive

2 The CD should autorun, if it doesn't, then just browse to the CD and double-click on PresentationPackage.html

3 Choose the presentation you wish to view by clicking on the name

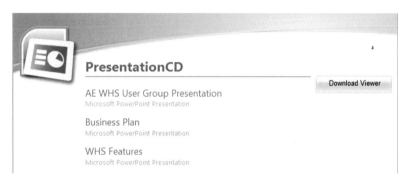

4 Enter the password to open the file, if prompted

5 If you don't know the password, as this is a presentation that someone else has given you, then you should contact them

6 When you have finished viewing the presentation, you can just remove the CD from the drive

Don't forget

You don't need to have PowerPoint installed on the computer you wish to view the presentation on if the CD has a link to the PowerPoint viewer included, for you to then click and download.

Beware

If the presentation needs a password in order to open it, and you don't know what it is, or you have forgotten it, there is no way to open the file.

Printing your Presentation

Printing a presentation is very easy, all you have to do is decide what, how and where you want to print.

Unlike previous versions of PowerPoint, 2010 automatically displays a preview of what you want to print on the right-hand side of the screen.

1 Press the File tab and choose Print

2 Select whether you want to print all slides, the current slide, or a selection of the slides

Don't forget

Make sure you have selected the printer you want to print to, and that it is switched on and has paper in it.

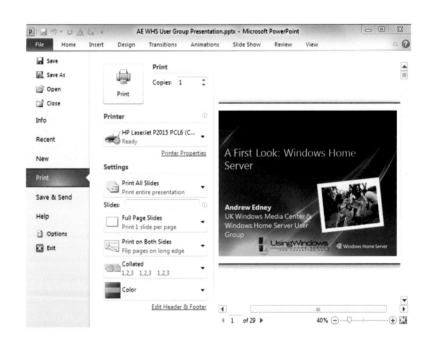

3 Select any other options

4 Click on Printer Properties, if you need to check settings on the printer itself

5 Click OK to begin printing

Print Options

PowerPoint gives you the ability to print four different types of output from your presentation. You can choose from these four types from the Print what drop-down box.

Slides
This option prints the slides exactly as they are on screen, depending on what other options may have been chosen.

Handouts
Handouts are prints of the slides designed specifically to give to people to take away from the presentation. You can print one slide per page, or a maximum of nine slides per page.

Notes pages
This option will print any of the speakers notes (if there are any) along with each slide.

Outline View
This option prints only the text from each slide – any graphics are not printed. This option can be very useful if you want to quickly, and easily, see what text is within the slides, without having to go through all the slides in depth.

PowerPoint Printing Options
You can set the way PowerPoint prints your presentations, from the Print settings within PowerPoint Options.

1 Click the File tab and select Options

2 Select Advanced

3 Check, or clear, the options you want to set

4 Click OK

Hot tip
When you choose to print 3 slides per page in Handouts mode, a number of blank lines are placed to the right of each slide, for note taking purposes.

Don't forget
If you choose to print in color, but you don't have a color printer, the prints will print out in similar quality to grayscale.

167

Beware
If you select Pure Black and White from the print options, certain features may not print, as the presentation will be printed using only bl and white, not gr

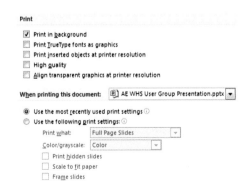

Print
☑ Print in background
☐ Print TrueType fonts as graphics
☐ Print inserted objects at printer resolution
☐ High quality
☐ Align transparent graphics at printer resolution

When printing this document: 📄 AE WHS User Group Presentation.pptx ▾

◉ Use the most recently used print settings ⓘ
◯ Use the following print settings: ⓘ
  Print what: Full Page Slides   ▾
  Color/grayscale: Color   ▾
  ☐ Print hidden slides
  ☐ Scale to fit paper
  ☐ Frame slides

Printer Properties

Before you actually start printing, it is a good idea to make sure that you have configured your printer exactly how you want it.

1 Press the File tab and choose Print

2 Select the printer you want to use and click Printer Properties

3 Properties you can change could include page order, paper type, print quality, and so on

Don't forget

Different printers have different properties that you can change. If in doubt about the printer's capabilities, consult the manual that came with your printer.

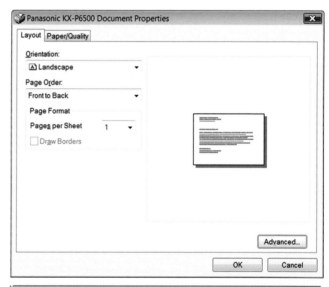

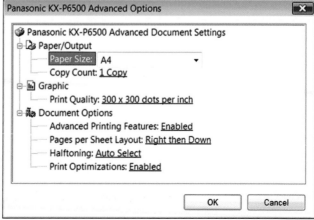

Publishing

You can publish any or all of your slides to a slide library, or any other location, by using the Publish Slides option in PowerPoint.

1 Press the File tab, highlight Save & Send, and select Publish Slides from the available options, then click the Publish Slides button

2 Tick the box, or boxes, for the slides you want to publish

3 Enter the location of where you want to publish and click Publish

Don't forget

If you want to publish to a SharePoint site, or document management server, make sure that they are available.

Hot tip

If you are saving to a library that requires files to be checked in or out, when you save the file to the server it is automatically checked out to you. You must check in the file before others can view or change it.

Don't forget

Make sure you have permission to the location or site you are trying to publish to.

Broadcasting your Slides

One of the new features of PowerPoint 2010 is the ability to broadcast your slides over the Internet, so that remote viewers can watch your presentation as you present it. All they need is access to the Internet and a URL, which you provide.

1. From the Slide Show tab, click the Broadcast Slide Show button

2. Click the Start Broadcast button, to use the PowerPoint Broadcast Service, or click Change Broadcast Service to use something different

3. You will need to enter your Windows Live ID credentials and then click OK to continue

4. You will now be connctected to the Broadcast Service and your presentation will be prepared – you can click cancel to stop at any time

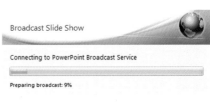

5 You will then be presented with a URL link that you must give to your remote viewers

6 Once the remote viewers have been given the URL link, you can click Start Slide Show to begin

7 Click the End Broadcast button to finish

Create a Video

Another new feature of PowerPoint 2010 is the ability to save your PowerPoint presentation as a video, so that you can distribute it in a number of different ways, and play it back on a variety of different devices, including a DVD player or a Zune device.

The video can include:

- all of the recorded timings, narrations and laser pointer gestures.

- all slides (apart from those you have hidden)

- all animations, transitions and media

To create a video of a presentation:

1 Press the File tab, highlight Save & Send and click on Create a Video

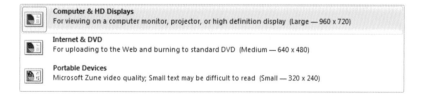

2 Choose what the video will be played on from the drop down list

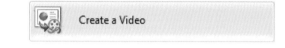

	Computer & HD Displays
	For viewing on a computer monitor, projector, or high definition display (Large — 960 x 720)
	Internet & DVD
	For uploading to the Web and burning to standard DVD (Medium — 640 x 480)
	Portable Devices
	Microsoft Zune video quality; Small text may be difficult to read (Small — 320 x 240)

3 Choose whether to include timings and narrations, from the drop down list

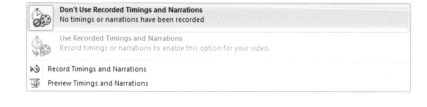

Don't Use Recorded Timings and Narrations
No timings or narrations have been recorded

Use Recorded Timings and Narrations
Record timings or narrations to enable this option for your video.

Record Timings and Narrations

Preview Timings and Narrations

Hot tip

If you are not sure where your viewers will be playing back the video from, you might want to consider making a video for each option.

4 If you haven't yet recorded any narrations or timings, you can do so now

5 Decide how many seconds each slide will appear for (the default setting is 5 seconds)

Seconds to spend on each slide: 05.00

6 When you are happy with your selections, click on the Create Video button

7 Choose a location to save the video files to, and click Save

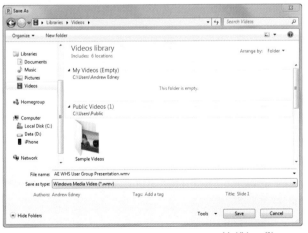

My Videos (1)
C:\Users\Andrew Edney

8 Distribute the video file

AE WHS User Group Presentation.wmv

173

Word Handouts

You can also create handouts in Microsoft Office Word. These are very useful if you want to share your presentation with others and have them either add comments to it, or for them to copy sections into other documents.

1 Press the File tab, highlight Save & Send and select Create Handouts, then click Create Handouts

You can then choose the desired page layout, including Notes next to slides or Outline only. Also whether or not to add the slides, or the actual Word document as well, or whether to include a link.

2 Select the desired page layout

3 Select whether to paste the slides or to paste a link to the slides, then click OK

A Microsoft Office Word document is then created from your presentation, using the parameters you selected. You can then email the Word document to anyone, or place it on a website.

Slide 14

Windows Home Server provides the ability to access and administer from a remote computer on the Internet from a web browser. This feature is disabled by default, but once it is enabled, the Windows Home Server can automatically configure your network to allow access to the remote access page so that you can get at your data wherever you might be.

12 Security

This chapter will guide you through some of the features that help you make your use of PowerPoint, and your presentations, more secure.

Using Passwords

If you want to stop others from modifying your presentation, or even opening it, you can set a password to protect it. Each time an attempt is made to open or modify the file (depending on what has been configured), a password must be entered.

Setting a Password

To set a password, make sure the presentation you want to protect is open. Click on the File tab and select Save As.

1. Click on the Tools button

2. Select General Options

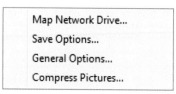

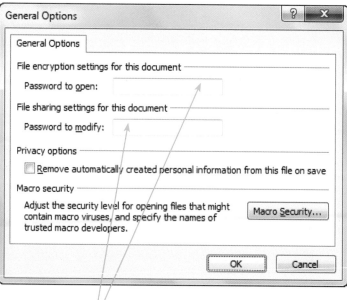

3. Enter a password to be used to either open the presentation, or modify the presentation (or both)

4 Check or clear the Remove automatically created personal information from this file on save box

5 Click OK to continue

6 You will then be prompted to confirm the password you just typed

Don't forget

Automatically created personal information includes such information as author, title, notes, XML information, and more, so you may not actually want that to be shared with others.

7 Click OK to finish

Using a Password Protected Presentation

Now that you have a password protected presentation, you will be asked to enter the password when you want to open it, modify it, or both (depending on what you selected previously).

Beware

If you set a password to stop someone from modifying your presentation, there is nothing to stop them from just copying the content into another presentation that they can modify!

1 Enter the password when prompted to open the file

Don't forget

Whatever you do, don't forget the password. If you do, you will not be able to open or edit the presentation again. If you write it down, make sure it is somewhere safe, but not obvious to anyone looking for it.

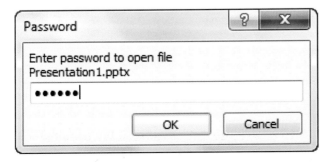

177

Restricting Permissions

You can also restrict people's ability to edit, copy, or print the presentation, using the Restrict Permission options.

Setting Permissions

1. Click on the File tab, then click Protect Presentation, then highlight Restrict Permission by People

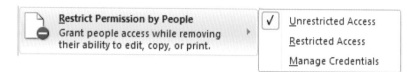

2. Choose to either leave the default Unrestricted Access selected, or select Restricted Access to specify a list of users and their permissions, or Manage Credentials to change the log-in credentials

3. Follow the steps to sign up for a free trial to the Microsoft Information Rights Management Service

4. Select Restrict permission to this presentation box, and enter email addresses in the Read and Change boxes, as required

5. Click on More Options to specify additional permissions

Available Permissions

Apart from changing a user's access level, additional permissions are available to be set, including:

- This presentation expires on – you can set a date when the presentation expires

- Print content – allows the presentation to be printed

In addition, you can add an email address where users can request additional permissions.

Don't forget

Make sure that you choose the permissions you want to use very carefully.

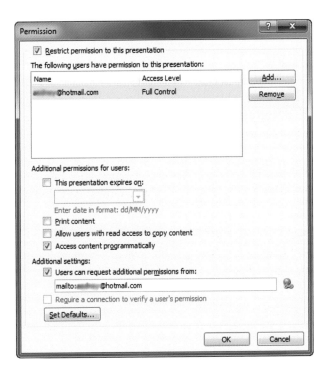

Beware

Users may still be able to circumvent some of these permissions using other software, or even just by copying the information by hand.

179

1 Change any permissions as required, then click OK

A presentation that has restricted permissions will display a Do Not Distribute bar at the top of the screen. Click on the Change Permissions button if you need to change any permissions.

Digital Signatures and IDs

PowerPoint gives you the ability to sign a presentation with a digital signature, also known as a digital ID. A digital signature is like your "real" signature, only it is invisible and is used to ensure the integrity of your presentation by assuring that the content has not been altered since you signed it.

Getting a Digital ID

If you don't already have a digital ID, you will need to either buy one or create one, depending on what you want to use it for.

 Choose Add a Digital Signature by pressing the Microsoft Office Button and highlighting Prepare

Add a Digital Signature
Ensure the integrity of the presentation by adding an invisible digital signature.

 Hot tip

If you want to sign presentations that will be shared with people for business reasons, you might want to consider obtaining an ID from a Microsoft partner, as it can be verified easily.

Select OK and then you will be presented with the choice to either Get a digital ID from a Microsoft partner, or Create your own digital ID. If you choose to get one from a Microsoft partner, you will be presented with a list of companies who can supply you with one. For now, select Create your own digital ID

Enter your details to create your digital ID. These must include your name, email address, organization (if applicable) and location. Then click on the Create button to finish

Signing a Presentation

Now that you have your digital ID, you can sign your presentation.

 Add a comment into the Purpose for signing this document box. Then click Sign to finish

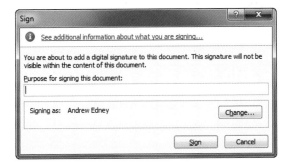

Viewing a Signature

You can view a signature on any signed presentation.

Choose View Signatures by clicking the File tab and then View Signatures

Signed Presentation
This presentation has been signed and marked as final. It should not be edited. If anyone tampers with this presentation, the signatures will become invalid.

View Signatures

Click on any valid signature and use the drop-down list to either view the signature details or remove the signature, if it is your signature

Don't forget

Before you can add a digital signature to your presentation, you must first save your presentation.

Hot tip

Adding a comment into the Purpose for signing this document box is useful to show others (and yourself later on) why you signed the presentation in the first place.

The Trust Center

The Trust Center is where the security and privacy settings for all Microsoft Office programs are managed.

 To access the Trust Center, click the File tab, followed by Options and then Trust Center

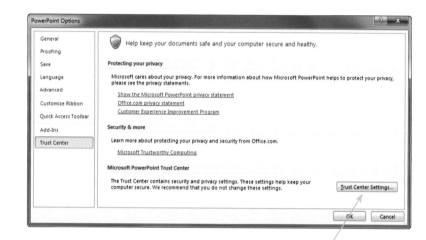

Then just click on the Trust Center Settings button

Add-ins

Add-ins are features that can enhance PowerPoint. These features could include templates, smart-tags and other useful additions. Here is where you can require that Add-ins are signed, or even disable all Add-ins.

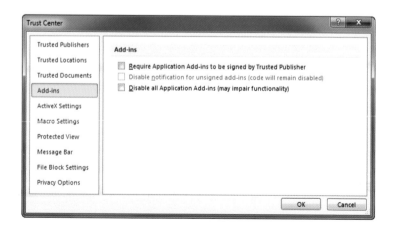

Message Bar

The Message Bar is very useful for warning you about content that PowerPoint has blocked. The Message Bar will appear under the Ribbon if a problem, or potential problem, arises. You can change the setting here if you do not want to see information about blocked content.

Beware

Always ensure that the Show the Message Bar in all applications when content has been blocked is enabled, as it is a very good idea to know if you might have a security problem.

Privacy Options

This is a useful set of options. Here you can enable or disable various privacy options, including allowing the searching of Microsoft Office Online for Help content, and even checking Microsoft Office documents that are from or link to suspicious websites. This option is very useful as it can be used to help protect you from potential phishing attacks.

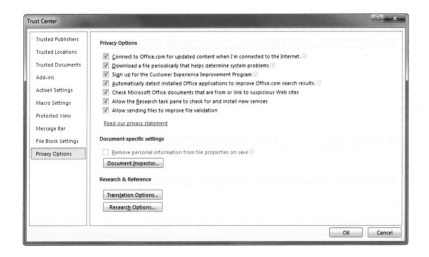

Don't forget

Some of the Privacy Options allow either downloads from Microsoft, or even uploading of information to Microsoft. Make sure you are happy to allow this before enabling those options.

Hot tip

It is a good idea to enable the Search Microsoft Office Online for Help content option, as this will give you access to up-to-date help documentation.

Macros

A macro is a piece of code that is used to automate frequently performed tasks.

Before enabling a macro, the Trust Center will perform a number of checks, including the following:

- The macro is signed by the developer, with a digital signature

- The digital signature is valid

- The digital signature has not expired

- The certificate that is associated with the digital signature has been issued by a reputable Certificate Authority (CA)

- The developer who signed the macro is a trusted publisher

If any problems are detected, the macro is automatically disabled, and you are notified of a potentially unsafe macro, and are also given the option of enabling it, if you are sure of what it will do and where it has come from.

Macros Settings

There are four macro settings to choose from. They are:

- Disable all macros without notification – all macros will be disabled and you will not be advised when this happens

- Disable all macros with notification – this is the default, and you will be advised when this happens so that you can choose to allow a macro if you are sure

- Disable all macros except digitally signed macros – any macros digitally signed by a trusted publisher will run, and all others will be disabled

- Enable all macros – this setting allows all macros to run

Changing Macro Settings

You can change settings that the Trust Center uses when detecting macros by first accessing the Trust Center.

Hot tip

You will probably find that the best setting to use is Disable all macros with notification. This will always give you the option of enabling the macro.

1 Choose Macro Settings from the Trust Center menu

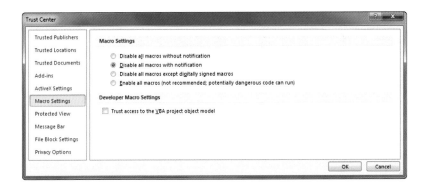

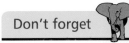

Don't forget

Never set Enable all macros, unless you are really, REALLY, sure!

2 Select the setting that you want to use

3 Check Trust access to the VBA project object model only if you are the developer and want to enable this trust

4 Click OK

ActiveX

ActiveX controls are components that can be anything, from a simple box to a toolbar, or even an application. ActiveX controls are commonly found on the Internet, and in various applications, including PowerPoint.

If the Trust Center detects a potentially unsafe ActiveX control, it is automatically disabled and you are given the option to enable it.

ActiveX Settings

There are four ActiveX settings to choose from. The three you are most likely to choose are:

- Disable all controls without notification – all controls are disabled and only a red X, or a picture of the control, will be displayed

- Prompt me before enabling all controls... – this is the default

- Enable all controls without restrictions... – allows any control to run

Changing ActiveX Settings

You can change the setting that the Trust Center uses for ActiveX controls by first accessing the Trust Center.

 Choose ActiveX Settings

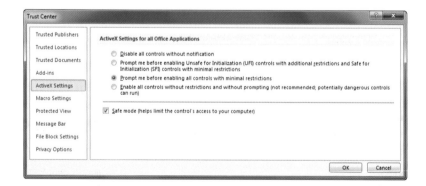

 Select the setting that you want to use and then click OK

Index

T